# Contextualizing New Plays

## Studies in Theatre Concepts, Forms, and Styles

FIRST EDITION

Scott R. Irelan and Anne Fletcher

cognella® | ACADEMIC PUBLISHING

Bassim Hamadeh, CEO and Publisher
Angela Schultz, Senior Field Acquisitions Editor
Michelle Piehl, Project Editor
Berenice Quirino, Associate Production Editor
Jess Estrella, Senior Graphic Designer
Trey Soto, Licensing Coordinator
Sue Murray, Interior Designer
Natalie Piccotti, Senior Marketing Manager
Kassie Graves, Director of Acquisitions and Sales
Jamie Giganti, Senior Managing Editor

Cover image: copyright © by SIU Department of Theater. Reprinted with permission.
Design image: Biboarchitect, "Theater Masks," http://www.clker.com/clipart-theatre-masks-19.html. Copyright in the Public Domain.

Printed in the United States of America

ISBN: 978-1-5165-2862-2 (pbk) / 978-1-5165-2863-9 (br)

# Contents

# CHAPTER 1

# Introduction

SCOTT R. IRELAN AND ANNE FLETCHER

*The broader one's understanding of the human experience, the better design we will have.*

Steve Jobs, *Wired*, February 1995

## Why Another Anthology of Plays?

Collecting plays that represent a variety of styles, forms, writers, characters, settings, and subject matter, all in the name of examining the human experience, can open the proverbial door to mining our material reality for ways to be more empathic, more creative, and perhaps even more humane. In the jammed marketplace of anthologies, though, the collection to be found in *Contextualizing New Plays* is unique in that it uses short (one act or less), unpublished, original plays as a way to discuss, even dissect, the **play script** (the blueprint for live theatrical performance). In compiling this collection, it was important to us to provide plays that not only acknowledged a long history of original play development in the

United States but also that looked back over a 3,000-year history of Western theatre for inspiration, all the while moving the debate regarding "Why Theatre?" into the future.

Given both the success of such recent original theatrical (or musical theatre) productions as *Hamilton, The Curious Incident of the Dog in the Night-Time,* and *August: Osage County,* and André Bishop's 2017 Tony Award statement that we are "in a golden age of American playwriting," it seemed appropriate to celebrate the original play process in anthology form at this time. Our secondary goal in doing so was to provide a way to introduce play-reading novices to a variety of **genres** (type or kind), **forms** (a play on the page), and **styles** (a play on the stage) in digestible "nuggets" while also pointing to longer, historical texts from the Western theatre tradition for further study. This approach should also serve teachers, professors, and professionals, as it should allow them to rethink their presumptions and find fresh creative voices; and in general, it should remind them of the fundamentals of theatre they were introduced to years ago.

## Why this Anthology?

This collection has several purposes beyond the broad ones mentioned above. First, the publisher commissioned us to provide nonmajor theatre students with a collection of plays that could not only compete with those perennial tomes in the existing marketplace but also be focused for specific use in introductory theatre classes. Second, given this charge, we were interested in providing a collection that would appeal to more than just the beginning theatre student. We worked hard to select texts that would be useful to acting students who are interested in challenging character-driven works; to beginning directing students; to nascent designers who are looking for imaginative texts on which to practice; to dramaturgs looking to work on original, short plays that have had limited stage time; and to the general lover of theatre who wants to read some interesting plays. Third, we had to make sure, in taking this approach, that we provided texts that addressed style, form, and genre relevant to the contemporary theatre. Given all of this, *Contextualizing New Plays* is meant as a viable alternative either to an anthology of full-length plays or to a random collection of separate acting edition scripts paired with a textbook or reading pack for use in theatre classes.

# The Pragmatics of Contextualizing

To our knowledge, there is no collection that takes our original, unpublished short play approach and includes discussion of thematic concerns while also incorporating critical theory, theatre history, and observations regarding style of production. Furthermore, there does not seem to be any collection of short plays intended for use in conjunction with study of longer scripts of the same forms, styles, or genres. For example, in the feminist plays by Kirsten Easton that have been included in *Contextualizing New Plays,* we point to her overlapping dialogue and overall concern with women's issues before we suggest other plays with similar attributes. In this case, for further reading we might offer up Henrik Ibsen's *A Doll's House*, or Sophie Treadwell's classic American Expressionist play *Machinal,* or the work of Susan Glaspell. By no means is this meant to be an exhaustive list; rather, it is a place to start with further research and discussion. We take this approach with each of the plays in this collection. The brief critical or historical commentaries provided for each included play also make this collection unique among the other anthologies in the marketplace of ideas. Again, it is this approach that also broadens the course appeal of *Contextualizing New Plays* beyond the introductory theatre class. The book might be used in conjunction with canonical plays in a theatre history class; utilized for play analysis; or even adopted in a playwriting class to visit how contemporary playwrights, both recently minted and experienced, tackle subject matter, style, and form. Directing students might find working with original pieces challenging, and—as directing assignments often require that students explore directing short plays—they might find these plays a welcome alternative to the ones more widely used. Moreover, anthologies seldom if ever include a pedagogical underpinning— that is, published suggestions for how to utilize the text. This, too, is distinctive in this collection. We have used this approach in our other two books, and it has met with great praise, so we continue it here.

This compilation of original, short plays is also meant to address common challenges that instructors face with regard to both the reading comprehension of contemporary learners and the waning attention span that has emerged in the social media age. Working at universities that boast flourishing playwriting programs, we have habitually incorporated the study of original works (both long and short plays) in our own classes—introduction to theatre, play analysis, dramaturgy, and theatre history. Our students have responded enthusiastically to the special experience of reading (in some instances, also seeing) and responding to inaugural printings or productions of original plays whose subject matter, characters, or even authors are often closer to the students in chronological age, life experience, and material concerns. Many of the plays included in this volume take on topics relevant to today's iGeneration as well as "millennials," all the while providing useful exemplars of traditional forms that date back to ancient Greek and Roman theatre. For example, Greg Aldrich's "The Ridiculously Sweet Dream Apartment" employs the three doors of classical farce but at the same time incorporates cell phone technology to create chaos and confusion in the play's action, which is set in the present. David Dudley's "Uprooting Oaks" was inspired by the senseless death of a young drummer in Carbondale, Illinois, who was struck by a stray bullet. The play addresses the contemporary "hot button" issues of guns and urban violence at the same time that it probes the ultimate universal concern of death. On a lighter note, Kiri Palm's "Unser Zuverlässiges Haus" casts the ubiquitous college experience of housing as **Expressionism** (a type of non-Realism that focuses on distortions that might be found in a dream).

On a pragmatic level (keeping in mind permissions, expenses, and the number of plays included in the collection), short plays were chosen in order reduce the overall number of pages needed to accomplish the study of structure and styles required by the contemporary theatre discipline. This approach was taken not only in an attempt to reduce the final cost but also, perhaps more importantly, to provide a fresh pedagogical approach to anthologized works.

Lastly, this collection's organizing principle(s) blends the consideration of basic theatrical concepts, dramatic forms, and styles of production with considerations of thematic concerns, dramatic criticism, and approaches to play reading through critical theory lenses. As such, we offer plays that deal both with timeless socio-cultural issues and with issues that have had a historical impact on the Western tradition. The issues taken on in this text include those of women and gender, HIV and AIDS, race and ethnicity, death and dying, and ecology, to name only a few.

# The Process of Reading this Anthology

Reading a play text in an anthology and seeing a play produced live are two radically different experiences. In fact, within our book *Experiencing Theatre* we talk at length about the major differences between reading a play on the page and seeing a live production of a play on stage. While we will not reproduce that content here, what follows is a condensed version of our larger conversation in that book.

Reading a play is an isolated experience that involves paying special attention to **plot** (ordered sequence of events), **character** (entities created to carry out plot action), and **idea** (meanings, messages, or thematic concerns). It is important to note that plot is different from **story**, which is the entire narrative of related incidents from which the writer chooses the plot. When seeing a play live in performance, we tend to rely on **language** (the primary way writers allow characters to communicate, both verbally and nonverbally), **music** (refers not only to the literal use of music but also to the pitch, rhythm, and tone of speech), and **spectacle** (all of the visual elements of a live production) to help us engage in that experience. Another important difference between reading a play in this anthology and seeing one staged live is that of form and style. Again, form refers to the way a text is written, and style (sometimes referred to as style of production) is how that written text looks on stage. It is always helpful for us to think of both form and style in terms of two broad categories: Realism and non-Realism.

**Realism** both as a form and as a style indicates a play where the illusion of everyday life is created. Also referred to as Illusionistic or Representational theatre, Theatrical Realism uses characters we might meet in our daily lives speaking in ways that are familiar to the given time period of the text wherein conversations revolve around topics such as intimate relationships, jobs, or even changing a tire on the side of the road. A key indicator that a text and the subsequent performance are Realism is that characters never directly speak to us as either readers or watchers.

They live in a self-contained world, and we are merely eavesdroppers. Referred to as non-Illusionistic or Presentational theatre, **non-Realism** makes no concerted effort to replicate daily life. While elements of daily life might be present, these sorts of pieces often have characters named for their function (for example, Mechanic, Daddy, Mommy), who speak directly to the reader/watcher (or at least acknowledge in some way that they are being read/watched) and are trapped in a plot that is not always grounded in what we might call "reality."

In between these dramatic forms (and styles) is a third option to consider: the hybrid play. A **hybrid play** is one that utilizes a mix of elements from both Realism and non-Realism. That is, perhaps a given play has a mix of characters with both proper names and functions as their names (for example, Willy and Woman) who sometimes engage in activities familiar to our daily lives (for example, eating steak) in a place that looks both familiar and strange at the same time (for example, a house in a growing neighborhood that has walls that characters can walk through). The play we have just described is Arthur Miller's time-honored *Death of a Salesman*.

So, what does all of this look like in *Contextualizing New Plays*? Let us take "Fireworks" as an example. We can immediately see from the Cast of Characters that each of the two characters has a formal, given name (Esperanza and Tony) and that both characters have jobs that we might experience in the world of our lives (professional dancer and established businessman). The setting information tells us that we are in a specific place and time that we can point to in history (Detroit on July 4, 2004). As the characters begin to talk, we hear a discussion that uses language that is of the era, if not of our day, about topics like "Where's the chip dip?" and "How was your day?"—both, perhaps, elements of daily life we can connect with on some level. Even the music choices match the era. In this case, then, the clues tell us that we are reading a piece of Realism. With this information, the acting student might be interested in diving further into the backgrounds of these two characters. The directing student might want to take on the project because of the intensity of the events. Designers not familiar with early 2000s fashion, music, and architecture might find some interesting representations of this time period. Dramaturgs have more than enough to start researching so that the world of the play can be both true to 2004 and inventive enough to capture a contemporary watcher. The general theatre lover will have certainly read an interesting play with an intense perception shift by the end. Each of the texts in *Contextualizing New Plays* provides this kind of layered consideration of concept, form, and style.

# The Pedagogy of Contextualizing

The pedagogy of *Contextualizing New Plays* is grounded in elements of constructivist education and blended with elements of Howard Gardner's multiple intelligences in that we encourage the use of these plays to actively build a "core of knowing" based on where readers are when they initially approach a given play text. To do this, we encourage active, experiential engagement with each text and its layers. We suggest that this be done through a variety of analysis and artistic response, discussion and debate. In order to support this, each brief introduction to the selected plays not only addresses elements of form and style but also offers pertinent framing material as a way of contextualizing the play text. In practical terms this means that we provide a beginning context from which to launch other learner-centered explorations of the material at hand. This is further supported at the end of each introduction by a list of longer works from theatre history that engage similar elements of form and style, theme and theory. At the end of each play text, we also include either a sample in-class activity or questions for further exploration. Ultimately, in designing *Contextualizing New Plays* we constantly sought to address this question: What are the different ways that readers can engage with each chosen text so that they can construct a core of knowing that will be applicable to larger, longer texts they may encounter in the future?

We turn now to a concrete example of how this pedagogical approach is embedded in the collection. We do this not to force a perspective on the works but rather as a way into using the text as a tool for building knowing. Take, for example, the included plays "The Bathing Suits" and "Fit" by Kirsten Easton. Here we suggest the context of feminist critical theory from which to view the plays as they are read. In doing this, then, we open up readers to the larger study of plays with similar form or style or theme or theoretical underpinning. In a similar way, a piece by George S. Kaufmann, a longer comedy like Moliere's *Tartuffe*, or self-identified farces like those by Alan Ayckbourn, or the ever-popular *Noises Off* by Michael Frayn might also pair well with "The Ridiculously Sweet Dream Apartment." David Crespy's "Stampede" opens the door for instructors to discuss longer AIDS/HIV plays such as *The Normal Heart, As Is,* or *The Baltimore Waltz*—all foundational plays within AIDS/HIV theatre history.

Since we practice experiential, activity-based learning in our classrooms, we include some suggestions for in-class activities with each of the plays. We do this not to be prescriptive but to offer a way into building "core knowing" with learners. Broad examples might include suggesting that aspiring designers create word clouds or search for inspirational images based on their initial reactions to the plays, or having actors make notes on what a play's characters reveal about themselves through dialogue, nonverbally in stage directions, and through what other characters say about them. Playwrights might take a line from the play and improvise some dialogue based on it in order to jump-start their own writing process. Directors and dramaturgs might work together to come up with a 30-second "elevator pitch" for the approach to a production of the play. You get the idea. In the end, we hope that you find our choices useful in your larger study of theatre and live performance.

# For Further Research

## PEDAGOGY

Armstrong, Thomas. *Multiple Intelligences in the Classroom.* 3rd edition. Alexandria, VA: Association for Supervision and Curriculum Development, 2009.

Brooks, Jacqueline Grennon, and Martin G. Brooks. *The Case for Constructivist Classrooms.* Alexandria, VA: Association for Supervision and Curriculum Development, 1993.

Gardner, Howard. *Frames of Mind: The Theory of Multiple Intelligences.* 2nd ed. New York: Basic Books, 1985.

## INTRODUCTION TO THE THEATRE

Fletcher, Anne, and Scott R. Irelan. *Experiencing Theatre.* Cambridge, MA: Hackett Publishing, 2015.

## DRAMATURGY

Irelan, Scott R., Anne Fletcher, and Julie Dubiner. *The Process of Dramaturgy: A Handbook.* Newburyport, MA: Focus Publishing, 2009.

## PLAY ANALYSIS AND DESIGN

Ingham, Rosemary. *From Page to Stage: How Theatre Designers Make Connections between Scripts and Images.* Portsmouth, NH: Heinemann, 1998.

## ACTING

Hagen, Uta. *Respect for Acting.* 2nd ed. Hoboken, NJ: Wiley, 2008.

**THEATRE HISTORY**

Brockett, Oscar G., and Franklin J. Hildy. *History of the Theatre*. 10th ed. Essex, UK: Pearson, 2007.

**DIRECTING**

Dean, Alexander, and Lawrence Carra. *Fundamentals of Play Directing*. 5th ed. Long Grove, IL: Waveland Press, 2009.

## CAUTION

Professionals and amateurs are hereby notified that all plays are under copyright and permission must be obtained to use them in any manner. All rights, including professional and amateur stage rights, motion picture, recitation, lecturing, public reading, radio broadcasting, television, video or sound recording, all other forms of mechanical or electronic reproduction, and the rights of translation into foreign languages, are strictly reserved. All inquiries concerning rights, including amateur rights, should be addressed to the writer or writer's agent.

# Image Credit

- biboarchitect, "Theater Masks," http://www.clker.com/clipart-theatre-masks-19.html. Copyright in the Public Domain.

# Bianca Sams

PLAYWRIGHT

## SUPERNOVA

### PRODUCTION HISTORY

SUPERNOVA has been seen at the Kennedy Center American College Theatre Region II Festival, been part of the Lewis & Clark College New Play Festival, was a finalist for the Minnesota Shorts Festival, and was staged at Ohio University's Midnight Madness Festival.

CAST OF CHARACTERS
LOU ANNE
MARY

SETTING—The Smith household's treehouse

### PLAYWRIGHT'S TECHNICAL NOTE

The piece requires a strong flashlight or light cues. This light is a major component of how Lou Anne communicates for much of the piece.

The house does not need to be totally black, but seeing the lone flashlight shatter the darkness can be immensely theatrical, especially in the beginning.

The actor playing Lou Anne has discretion on the flashlight momentum, using it to punctuate thoughts, emotions, when she is listening and when she is not. What is in the script is an approximation, but clicking should definitely be happening throughout Mary's lines as well.

## About the Playwright

Bianca Sams is a writer/actor hailing from the San Francisco Bay Area. Her plays are lyrical investigations of found stories from either today's headlines or the pages of history. Her work often asks audiences to face their own complex love affair with misery. She recently finished her MFA in Playwriting at Ohio University, first receiving her BFA from New York University's Tisch School of the Arts. While studying at Tisch, she earned the distinction of being its first triple major (Acting, Dramatic Writing, and Africana Studies). Her awards and honors include Ingram New Works Fellow (Nashville Repertory Theatre), Warner Brothers TV Writing Workshop, KCACTF Lorraine Hansberry Award (second place), Rosa Parks Award (second place), Kennedy Center/Eugene O'Neill New Play Conference Fellow, Jane Chambers Student Playwright Award/ATHE (second place in 2013 and 2014), Scott McPherson Playwright Award, The Playwright Center Core Apprentice (2014), Playwright Foundation BAPF (finalist), Eugene O'Neill NPC (semifinalist), TRI Research Fellowship at Ohio State University, and T. S. Eliot Acting Fellowship. She is now pursuing a career in film and television in Los Angeles, where she worked as a staff writer on the CBS/WB show *Training Day*. She was also included in the Tracking Board's Young & Hungry List for 2016, an annual index of the top 100 young writers to watch.

# Form and Style

"Supernova" was first written as a 10-minute play for Ohio University's Midnight Madness Festival. It is currently being turned into a full-length play with the same title. "Supernova," as presented here, centers on a young girl who loves both astronomy and her late father. She is currently struggling with her own mortality. In this case, playwright Sams renders the story of Lou Anne and her mother Mary in the form of Theatrical Realism. Some clues to this come when the writer tells us the formal names of each character, states their positions in life (daughter and mother), and reveals to us background information about their life together through dialogue (known as **exposition**). What particularly interests us about the play is the way that Sams both introduces us to Lou Anne's Asperger's Syndrome (AS) and ultimately portrays the disorder through Lou Anne.

Asperger's Syndrome derives its name from pediatrician Hans Asperger. In 1944, the Viennese doctor noticed a pattern of behavior in many of his male patients. He observed that several of the boys had normal language development and normal (if not enhanced) intelligence levels, but that these same boys were not especially skilled in social situations, were not able to communicate well with other people, and often had bad coordination skills. As research into these aspects continued over time, doctors other than Asperger were able to confirm that, more often than not, children with the syndrome were socially awkward and physically clumsy with strong verbal expression skills. Until recently, AS was considered its own condition with its own set of diagnostic indicators. In 2013, however, the American Psychological Association changed the classification of AS in *The Diagnostic and Statistical Manual of Mental Disorders, Fifth Edition* (DSM-5) to a special type of autism. As such, those diagnosed with AS are often referred to as being "on the autism spectrum." The primary factors currently used to diagnose AS are impairment in social communication and social interaction, along with repetitive behavior. While certainly a more multifaceted syndrome than that, in contemporary times Asperger's—whether good or bad—has become shorthand for a hyper-focused, socially awkward, clever person who perhaps feels like an outsider.

As you read "Supernova," take extra care to consider how Sams has created the character of Lou Anne. In fact, see if you can identify how the writer has incorporated some of the better-known Asperger's behaviors into the play. These might include—but are not limited to—impairment in using nonverbal cues like eye contact; a fascination with maps, patterns, and routes; difficulty with peer relationships, preferring adults over children; a preoccupation with certain objects; an amassed library of facts; and repetitive mannerisms, movements, or physicalizations. We recommend a little more research on your part to enhance your appreciation of the play, as we have provided only the briefest of brief introductions to the syndrome.

# Plays for Further Study

When thinking about how Asperger's Syndrome has been rendered in other dramatic writing, what first comes to mind is the television series *Parenthood*. Though it is not a play for further study, watching a few scenes where the character Max interacts with others might be useful in imagining how Lou Anne functions on a day-to-day basis. That said, there are many good plays for you to read and research. *The Curious Incident of the Dog in the Night-Time,* adapted for theatre by Simon Stephens, follows the socially ill-equipped Christopher and his exceptional work as he goes about solving the murder of his neighbor's dog. Ken LaZebnik's *Theory of the Mind* shares what happens when Bill, a high-school senior on the autism spectrum, misreads almost every social cue a girl, Hilo, gives him as they go out on a date. *Soot and Spit* by Charles Mee looks at the life of deaf artist James Castle, who was quite possibly on the autism spectrum. Mark St. Germain's *Dancing Lessons* introduces us to Ever, a geoscientist with Asperger's, who is interested in receiving dance lessons from a Broadway dancer so that he can survive an evening at an awards dinner. The dancer, Senga, who lives in Ever's apartment building, is recovering from a possible career-ending injury. The meeting of the two is fortuitous.

In broadening our scope from Asperger's Syndrome to other topics covered by what the industry calls disability theatre, we recommend looking at *Distracted* by Lisa Loomer, *The Boys Next Door* by Tom Griffin, *Sweet Nothing in My Ear* by Stephen Sachs, and *The Cripple of Inishmaan* by Martin McDonagh. *Distracted* takes ADD/ADHD as its topic of exploration, while *The Boys Next Door* is interested in exploring developmental and mental health. Deaf culture is what drives the narrative of *Sweet*

*Nothing in My Ear.* Martin McDonagh's *The Cripple of Inishmaan* takes us into the world of Billy, who is living with physical challenges, and his dreams of escaping Inishmaan to become a famous actor.

## CAUTION

# SUPERNOVA

LOU ANNE—14-year-old girl with mild Asperger's Syndrome
MARY—Her mother

SETTING—The Smith household's treehouse

**AT RISE:** Click. Click. Click. Click. Click. A lone flashlight clicking on and off pierces the darkness in the theatre. We see LOU ANNE sitting cross legged in a "tree house" feverishly signaling the fifth star to the right in Gemini. Click. Click. Click. Click. We hear a voice in the darkness yelling up to LOU ANNE. It's her mother MARY.

MARY (O.S.)
Lou-la-belle, your friend Bryce is about to leave. Come say goodbye—I mean come say see you later to him—

(LOU ANNE clicks faster. Click. Click. Click. Click. Click. Click.)

MARY (O.S.)
Oh this is ridiculous! Lou Anne Marie Smith you get down here right this instant. I know you're upset but that is no reason to be rude to a house full of guests—

(Click. Click. Click. Click. Click. Click.)

MARY (O.S.)
Lou Anne!
I know you hear me. Don't make come up there.

(Click. Click. Click. Click. Click. Click. Click.)

Bianca Sams, "Supernova." Copyright © 2014 by Bianca Sams. Reprinted with permission.

MARY (O.S.)

You know I hate when you—Are you really gonna—Fine—
Here I come.
Shit, aw hell, damnation!

LOU ANNE

Someone's having a swearfest—

MARY (O.S.)

And you're gonna hear a hell of a lot more if you don't bring your tail, ouch,
ouch. Dang it.

LOU ANNE

You okay?

(Click. The flashlight stops in the on position sweeping across the floor.
It allows us to see MARY for the first time. SHE's hobbling into the "tree
house.")

MARY

Yeah, just banged my daggone knee. Oh. Dear God that was a rough ride! I
swear I don't understand the fascination you and your father have with this
mangled mess of a tree house.

LOU ANNE

Well, I am my father's daughter.

(Click. Click. Click. Click.)

MARY

I didn't mean—

LOU ANNE

It's. It's fine.

(Click. Click. Click. Click.)

MARY

Lou-la-belle. I know you ain't happy about all this but I thought maybe you needed the support of your friends to help you make it through all this—

(Click. Click.)

LOU ANNE

Well, I don't—

(Click. Click. Click. Click.)

MARY

Well, they want to support you anyway.

(Click. Click. Click. Click. Click. Click. Click. Click. Click. Click.)

We all do. We all just love you to pieces and want to do anything we can to um make you comfortable and strong enough for tomorrow—Lou lou, are you crying?

(Click. Click. Click. Click. Click. Click. Click. Click.)

LOU ANNE

Can't you go! Go back to your weirdo "support" party and leave me alone.

(Click. Click. Click. Click. Click.)

MARY

What's so weird about your friends and family wanting to be there for you?

LOU ANNE

Just forget it—

MARY

No, I won't. I spent all week planning this surprise. Your grandma came from the nursing home. Your friends are here on a school night. Why is that so weird?

LOU ANNE

It's weird because all them people are here to say goodbye before the supernova. It's creepy morbidity that's why!

(Click. Click. Click. Click. Click. Click. Click. Click. Click. Click.)

MARY

Before the what? Would you stop that!

(Click. Click. Click. Click. Click. Click. Click. Click. Click. Click. Click. Click. Click. Click. Click.)

LOU ANNE

No time to stop. No time ...

(Click. Click. Click. Click. Click. Click. Click. Click. Click. Click. Click. Click. Click. Click. Click.)

MARY

Baby, baby, it's O.K. It's—

### LOU ANNE

It's not O.K.! I wish everyone would stop saying that! My hydrogen is depleted and tomorrow I'm gonna become an eskimo nebula or supernova all together and and and—

(Click. Click. Click. Click. Click. Click. Click. Click. Click.)

### MARY

Breathe! Lou-la-belle, just slow breathe in and slow breathe out! Slow breathe—

### LOU ANNE

I know how to breathe, Mom! You don't have to control my breathing too!

### MARY

I wasn't trying to—

(Click. Click. Click. Click. Click. Click. Click. Click. Click. Click. Click. Click. Click. Click.)

I just—
Can't you just talk to me?!

### LOU ANNE

Why, so you can just override what I want and tell me how to think?! How to feel? You've managed every day of my life. You're even controlling the way I exit it!

### MARY

Lou Anne, I'm just looking out for your best interest.

### LOU ANNE

No, you're looking out for yours.

MARY

They said it was a 50% chance, Lou ...

LOU ANNE

Which means a 50% chance that it won't work. A 50% chance that they will open up my dome tomorrow and turn me into Nebula 2392.

(Click. Click. Click. Click. Click. Click. Click. Click. Click. Click. Click. Click. Click. Click. Click.)

MARY

Turn you into what?

LOU ANNE

NGC 2392. Oh forget it. Dad would understand—

(Click. Click. Click. Click. Click. Click. Click. Click. Click. Click. Click. Click. Click. Click. Click. Click. Click. Click. Click. Click.)

MARY

No, please.
I'm trying here.
I know I'm not science-cool like your dad but, I'm trying. So please.
Just explain it to me. Show me!

(LOU ANNE turns out the light and points with her finger into the night sky.)

LOU ANNE

She's there ... five stars to the right in Gemini.

MARY

Wow, she's beautiful. Brilliant.

LOU ANNE

Can't you see she's fading?! Her hydrogen's almost depleted! She's already shedding her outer most layers, if she's lucky she'll become a dwarf star, a shadow of herself, until she slowly glows no more! Or or or she'll supernova in one huge burst for a quick finish! But, either way she is fragile like us, born, living, but ultimately mortal.

(Click. Click. Click. Click. Click. Click. Click. Click. Click. Click.)

MARY

But, she's still there, Lou Anne. We can see her.

(LOU ANNE slams her flashlight down in the on position.)

LOU ANNE

Mom! The light we see isn't even her! Just her reflection that has traveled through the vast universe and finally down to us. Her light echoes out into the darkness of the void traveling the speed of light to finally pass us on our tiny little spec called earth, millions of light years away but, even after she's gone … her light will continue long after.

(Click. Click. Click. Click. Click. Click. Click. Click. Click. Click. Click. Click. Click. Click. Click.)

MARY

There is a 50% chance, Lou Anne … A 50% chance that they will be able to remove the mass. A 50% chance that you'll be fine for decades, maybe more—

LOU ANNE

Which means there is also a 50% chance of me becoming a dwarf star drooling shell of myself, slowly fading into nothing, leaving you to clean up my poop and feed me! Or maybe I will supernova and just go out in one bang tomorrow. Poof.

MARY

It's still a chance—

(Click. Click. Click. Click. Click.)

LOU ANNE

Dad had a 90% chance.

(Click. Click. Click. Click. Click.)

MARY

That's not the same thing at all … not even remotely!

(MARY takes the flashlight from LOU ANNE.)

LOU ANNE

He finds one tiny little discolored speck on the back of his neck one day and the next it's pills, weight loss, and chemo! One day he's fine and the next poof! Supernova. If he couldn't survive something tearing at the outside of his body, then how am I supposed to survive having my dome ripped open?

MARY

You're not your father. It's not the same situation!

LOU ANNE

I am my father's daughter. He didn't make it. I might not either.

MARY

Stop this, okay! You've got to be positive here. It's a good chance that—

LOU ANNE

Chances are chances, Mom, not guarantees. I got to shine my light while I still can. Maybe it will echo out and linger ...

(LOU ANNE takes the flashlight back.)

(Click. Click. Click. Click. Click. Click. Click. Click. Click. Click. Click. Click. Click. Click.)

MARY

Lou-la-belle, please—Just stop—
Lou—

LOU ANNE

No time left. No time. I got to shine while I still can!

(Click. Click. Click. Click. Click. Click. Click. Click. Click. Click.)

MARY

Then why why why waste it out into the dark sky, huh? Why not shine it on me? Shine it on on on all your friends in there. Let it live in us. We can carry your light.

LOU ANNE

Until your light goes out that is! Dad left you and me to carry his light and now I'm almost gone! Which means his light has nearly faded. Grandma's already half way in the grave and what ... You've got maybe 5–10 more years left?

MARY

HEY! I'm not that old!

LOU ANNE

I'm just saying … when you're gone and they're gone … so am I. It's not enough. People are not enough.

(Click. Click. Click. Click. Click. Click. Click. Click. Click. Click. Click. Click. Click. Click. Click.)

MARY

If, the worst happens tomorrow. And that is a big IF. It's better to shine your light on those that love you. At least down here we are sure to see the light.

(Click. Click. Click. Click. Click. Click. Click. Click. Click. Click.)

But, you're shining yours out into the vast nothing of the universe on the off chance that there is someone on the other end to recognize what they are seeing.

(Click. Click. Click. Click. Click.)

At least with us there is an 100% chance that it will be recognized. You have a 100% chance of shining bright in my heart until the moment I breathe my last and I come to meet you and your father on the other side. No, that's a guarantee!

(Click. Click. Click.)

But, Lou Anne. Your father didn't just come hide himself away.

(Click. Click.)

He spent every waking moment with you and me. He lived every second of every day of his life to the fullest. So be his daughter! Come down with me and come back inside. Live for today and leave tomorrow to tomorrow.

(Beat.)

(Click. Click. Click. Click. Click. Click. Click. Click. Click. Click.)

MARY

Ok. Well.
If you change your mind ... I'll be inside waiting. I love you.

(Click. Click. Click. Click. Click. Click. Click. Click. Click. Click.)

LOU ANNE

Mom?!

MARY

Yeah, Lou-la-belle?

LOU ANNE

I love you too ...

(LOU ANNE points the flashlight on her mother.)

(Click.)

(Slow fade to Blackout.)

**END OF PLAY**

# Group Discovery: An Exercise on Disability Theatre

1. Break into groups of four to six.
2. Using a preferred web browser, search *disability* and *theatre.*
3. From professional theatre productions of *disability theatre,* find one or two production images that intrigue you.
4. Visit the site of the theatre company that produced the play that is being shown in the image(s) you have chosen.
5. Share with everyone what you learned about the play and the theatre, and why the writer created the play.

# For Further Research

Bieber, Ruth. *Disability Theatre from the InsideOut.* UK: Chipmunka Publishing, 2012.

Hunter, Kelly. *Shakespeare's Heartbeat: Drama Games for Children with Autism.* London: Routledge, 2015.

Johnston, Kirsty. *Disability Theatre and Modern Drama: Recasting Modernism.* New York and London: Bloomsbury Methuen Drama, 2016.

———. *Stage Turns: Canadian Disability Theatre.* Montreal, QC, and Kingston, Ontario: McGill-Queen's University Press, 2012.

Nowinski, Deborah E. *Your Role in Inclusion Theatre: The Guide to Integrating Actors with Disabilities and Nondisabled in Your Theatre and Classes.* CreateSpace Independent Publishing Platform, Amazon Inc., 2015.

# CHAPTER 3

# Thomas Michael Campbell

PLAYWRIGHT

## dREAMtRIPPIN'

©2013 Thomas Michael Campbell

## PRODUCTION HISTORY

Nominated for the John Cauble Playwriting Award for Outstanding Short Play, dREAMtRIPPIN' has received several academic and professional stagings. The first academic production was staged in February 2007 in Carbondale, Illinois. That production was remounted at Marquette University in January 2008. The play received a staged reading at the Kennedy Center for the Performing Arts in April 2008. Ben Jacobs directed the play at Goshen College's Umble Center in October 2008, and Brenna Larsen staged the play at the University of Northern Colorado in December 2012.

Professional productions of dREAMtRIPPIN' include the July 2007 staging at HB Studio in New York City, the June 2008 staging at The Tre Stage Theatre in Hollywood, California, and the April 2011 staging at CHAW/Taffety Punk Theater Company in Washington, D.C.

CAST OF CHARACTERS
  STEVEN
  KAREN

SETTING—A variety of places along the road. Present day.

# About the Playwright

Originally from the Denver area, Thomas Michael Campbell is an assistant professor of Communications and Theatre Arts at the University of Wisconsin-Sheboygan. He is also the director of University Theatre, the campus's theatre program. Campbell earned his BFA in Playwriting/Directing from the University of Wyoming in 2003; his MFA in Playwriting from Southern Illinois University (SIU) in 2007; and his PhD in Speech Communication/Theatre also from SIU in 2013, specializing in dramaturgical studies. His dissertation, entitled *Alcoholism on the American Stage: De-Stigmatizing Socially Constructed Depictions of the Alcoholic Through Performance,* is an interdisciplinary approach to play analysis and script interpretation. His research focuses on how depictions/portrayals of alcohol abuse/dependency on the American stage can either act to perpetuate or to subvert stigmas and stereotypes associated with alcoholism. His plays have been seen in cities across the country, including Los Angeles, Seattle, Denver, and Chicago; at the HB Studio in New York City; at The John F. Kennedy Center for the Performing Arts; and with Taffety Punk at the Capitol Hill Arts Workshop (CHAW) in Washington, D.C. Other of his playwriting credits include *The Bearer of Bad News* (1999), *The Four Horsemen* (2000), *Moon Garden* (2002), *American Shih-Tzu* (2003), *Paralysis* (2005), *Awkward Silence* (2006), *The Highwayman* (2007), *Risata, Sciocco … Risata!* (2011), and *Descartes à la Mode* (2014).

# Form and Style

Campbell's play is a great example of a hybrid play that blends expected elements of Theatrical Realism with those of Surrealism. In this case, the play is more an example of non-Realism than Realism, because it relies on the attributes of Surrealism more than it relies on those of Realism. But what are those attributes? There are two root words that tell us much about **Surrealism** as a form and a style. The first is from the French word *sur,* meaning "above," and the second is from the French word *réalisme,* meaning just that: "realism." Thus, *sur-réalisme* is interested in looking at those things above or beyond the realism of our daily lives. Interestingly, Surrealism remains one of the more codified influences on contemporary theatre and live performance. When it first emerged in the early 1920s, theatre practitioners working within the movement were interested in rebelling against the rational, ordered restrictions of Realism in order to better explore the human condition based on subconscious imagery as discussed by Freud. Several of the early plays use quick scenes that have no sense of being ordered in a rational manner. This often leads to confusing storylines, if not disjointed or illogical plots. Writers, designers, and directors working within Surrealism are also interested in leveraging the dream state to provide a collection of characters, whether real or imagined, who can meet up only in a fantastical place (such as the subconscious mind).

A closer reading of dREAMtRIPPIN' also reveals that fundamental elements of comedy have influenced the way Campbell shares the adventures of Karen and Steven with us. From the ancient Greek *komos,* meaning "merry-making," comedy has its roots in the amusement that can come from deviating from the norm. Though there are several genres of comedy now, the basic elements are the same as they were thousands of years ago. The **comic premise** is the idea that the world of the play is out of balance somehow. It is the struggle to bring that world back into balance that drives any comedy. In many cases, the laws of nature are suspended (for example, gravity works only sometimes), the social order is disrupted (for example, the lower-class characters rule over the upper-class characters), and the foolish lengths that humans go to sometimes are accentuated (for example, withholding sex from soldiers to end war). Inconsistencies and incongruities are those out-of-place surprises that often provide amusement as the plot unfolds (for example, mistaken identity of characters). The end of the play rebalances the out-of-balance world we started with in the first place.

# Plays for Further Study

*The Breasts of Tiresias* is the play that launched Surrealism in theatre and live performance. In this play, writer Guillaume Apollinaire presents us with a woman, Thérèse, who decides to become a man, Tiresias, to obtain power in the male-dominated culture. Over the course of the play, Thérèse's breasts float away as she becomes a man, Thérèse-now-Tiresias then serves in parliament, and her ex-husband gives birth to over 40,000 children. In *The Mysteries of Love: A Surrealist Drama,* playwright Roger Vitrac juxtaposes unlike elements both in form and in content to question the notion of "romance." For an example of how Surrealism looks in motion pictures, we suggest *Spellbound* with Gregory Peck and Ingrid Bergman. Peck's character has amnesia and Bergman's psychoanalyst character uses Freudian techniques to unpack his subconscious; there are some rather vivid Surrealist sequences, complete with faceless men, floating eyeballs, and melting scenery.

In thinking about examples of comedy for further study, we turn first to the Ancient Greeks and Romans. *Lysistrata* by Aristophanes is an antiwar play that poses the question "What if the women of the city refused sex until fighting ended?" Sexual jokes, satire, and wordplay are what keep the plot moving. Plautus's *The Brothers Menaechmi* explores what happens when twins separated in childhood, one Menaechmus of Epidamnus and the other Menaechmus of Sosicles, arrive in the same region. Since they look alike, there are many laughable moments of mistaken identity before they eventually recognize each other. Years later, Shakespeare emerged as a master of the romantic comedy. This was helped, of course, by the fact that many Elizabethans preferred romantic comedy to other forms. One of our favorites is *As You Like It.* In this play, along with many others in this genre, the heroine (Rosalind) disguises herself as a man for part of the play and is much more crafty and cunning than any man in the world of the play. *The Movie Game* by Adam Hummel received the Mark Twain Award for Comedy. In it, Jack Goldberg sees a therapist to the stars who prescribes a unique therapy: performing the lead in his own romantic comedy.

## CAUTION

*Professionals* and amateurs are hereby notified that all plays are under copyright and permission must be obtained to use them in any manner. All rights, including professional and amateur stage rights, motion picture, recitation, lecturing, public reading, radio broadcasting, television, video or sound recording, all other forms of mechanical or electronic reproduction, and the rights of translation into foreign languages, are strictly reserved. All inquiries concerning rights, including amateur rights, should be addressed to the writer or writer's agent.

# Image Credit

- Source: Dramatists Guild.

# dREAMtRIPPIN'

CAST OF CHARACTERS
    STEVEN—A businessman, young
    KAREN—A woman from his office, younger

    SETTING—A variety of places along the road. Present day.

**AT RISE:** Lights come up on the interior of the car, mid-afternoon. KAREN sits in the passenger seat asleep. STEVEN drives. After a moment, SHE stirs and raises her head, looking out her window to survey the atmosphere. Silence. KAREN speaks to STEVEN still staring out the window.

KAREN

Where are we?

STEVEN

Nowhere.

KAREN

We have to be somewhere.

STEVEN

Not if you're driving through ... this. Vast areas of nothingness out here.

KAREN

I've never driven out here.

STEVEN

We should have come through at night.

KAREN

It doesn't look so bad.

STEVEN

If you like corn.

KAREN

There's a silo. That's different.

STEVEN

Nice try. Trust me, this is just as visually stimulating in the dark.

(Beat. There is a quiet, rhythmic thumping. Beat.)

KAREN

Do you hear that?

STEVEN

Hear what?

KAREN

A thumping.

STEVEN

The car?

KAREN

Maybe ... More like a beat. A rhythm.

(Silence. THEY listen.)

                                    STEVEN
I don't hear anything.

                                    KAREN
I guess it's gone.

                                    STEVEN
Maybe it's all in your head.

                                    KAREN
Wouldn't surprise me ...

        (THEY drive on.)

You've been out here before?

                                    STEVEN
Last year ... The Omegatech Conference.

                                    KAREN
Right ...

        (Long pause.)

                                    STEVEN
You okay?

                                    KAREN
Yeah. Still trying to wake up. Why?

                                    STEVEN
You seem distracted.

                    KAREN
Just thinking.

                    STEVEN
Anything specific?

                    KAREN
Not really.

                    STEVEN
You were making noises earlier.

                    KAREN
Noises?

                    STEVEN
I think you were dreaming. It was funny. They were like whimpers. It was cute.

                    KAREN
My dreams are funny and cute?

        (The car drives on. Beat.)

                    STEVEN
Karen ... ?

                    KAREN
Steven.

                    STEVEN
We should talk.

KAREN

About what?

STEVEN

What we're doing. At least, what we're about to do?

KAREN

It's a conference. No big deal. We go, we schmooze, say thanks, come home.

STEVEN

No. I mean us. You and me. Your feelings for me.

KAREN

What do you mean?

STEVEN

Don't play dumb, Karen. I'm an adult. I can handle it.

KAREN

I don't know what you're talking about.

STEVEN

You're only twenty-three years old.

(THEY drive.)

You only think you love me, Karen.

(KAREN, who has been looking out her window the entire time, suddenly wakes up. SHE has been dreaming. Her awakening is abrupt and grabs STEVEN's attention. HE addresses her without any knowledge of their previous conversation.)

Good, you're awake. You were snoring.

                        KAREN
What?

                        STEVEN
It was starting to bug me. I thought about turning up the radio, but I didn't want
to wake you up.
                        KAREN
     (Coming into full conscious)
Where are we?


                        STEVEN
Nowhere.


                        KAREN
We have to be somewhere.


                        STEVEN
Not if you're driving through vast areas of nothingness!


                        KAREN
Right … the corn.


                        STEVEN
There's a lot of it.


                        KAREN
Except for that silo.


                        STEVEN
Yeah. Except for that.


     (Long pause.)

                    STEVEN
I've been thinking ...

                    KAREN
Yes?

                    STEVEN
We should talk.

                    KAREN
        (Hesitates. Beat.)
About the conference.

                    STEVEN
Um ... yes.

                    KAREN
        (Looking back out her window)
We'll go, we'll schmooze, say our thank you's, and come home.

                    STEVEN
What about—

                    KAREN
The conference doesn't start for two days.

                    STEVEN
A day and a half.

                    KAREN
We'll be fine.

STEVEN

Sure ...

(Pause.)

KAREN

What time is it?

STEVEN

Afternoon.

KAREN

I can drive if you want.

STEVEN

There's a place up ahead. I thought we'd stop there for the night.

KAREN

Where?

STEVEN

Up ahead.

KAREN

I thought we were still in—

STEVEN

We're not.

KAREN

It looks like—

STEVEN

Like I said, everything's pretty much the same.

KAREN

Right ...

    (Beat.)

Was I dreaming? Earlier. Was I making funny noises?

STEVEN

What kind of noises?

KAREN

I don't know ... like whimpering.

STEVEN

You whimper when you're awake.

KAREN

No, I don't.

STEVEN

You're kind of whiney, Karen.

KAREN

I am not whiney!

STEVEN

You can't say you're not whiney in a whiney voice.

KAREN

(Noticing the speedometer)
You're going a little fast there, aren't you?

STEVEN

We're making great time.

KAREN

It's going to be pointless if we don't get there at all.

STEVEN

Settle down. I know what I'm doing.

KAREN

It's a little fast is all.

STEVEN

You can drive however you want when you're behind the wheel, and I won't say a thing. 'Kay, Grandma?

KAREN

Fine. But you better—

(Looking ahead.)

—Steve, watch out—!

(KAREN startles herself awake, while STEVEN sits as if nothing has happened. Again, SHE was dreaming. This time her heart is racing, and SHE's slightly short of breath. STEVEN looks at her.)

                    STEVEN

You okay?

                    KAREN

I was dreaming.

                    STEVEN

Obviously. You look like you just saw a ghost.

                    KAREN

Sorry.

                    STEVEN

You don't need to apologize to me.

                    KAREN

Sorry …

                    STEVEN

What were you dreaming about?

                    KAREN

We got in a car wreck.

                    STEVEN

Really? Suck.

                    KAREN

You were driving too fast.

        (STEVEN looks at her. HE slows down.)

STEVEN

Better?

KAREN

Yes. Thank you.

STEVEN

We should probably figure out where we're going to stop for the night.

KAREN

We could stop here.

STEVEN

Here?

KAREN

It looks nice. Right? Don't you think it looks … nice?

(Silence. After a moment...)

STEVEN

You doing better?

KAREN

Yeah. I've been having weird dreams lately.

STEVEN

What kind of dreams?

KAREN

(SHE looks at him)
You'll make fun of me if I tell you.

                        STEVEN
I'll make fun of you if you don't.


                        KAREN
     (Beat)
They're like—I don't know ... Really vivid ... Sometimes, they come true.


                        STEVEN
Like premonitions?


     (SHE nods. STEVEN bites his lip.)


                        KAREN
See, I knew it. I totally knew it.


                        STEVEN
I didn't say anything.


                        KAREN
You didn't have to.


                        STEVEN
I'm sorry.


                        KAREN
No, you're not. You're making fun of me, and you're totally okay with it.


                        STEVEN
I shouldn't have asked.

KAREN

No, you shouldn't have.

        (KAREN turns back to her window to look out at the vast nothingness.
        Silence.)

STEVEN

I didn't mean to make you mad.

KAREN

        (Not looking at him)
You didn't.

STEVEN

Then why won't you look at me?

        (No response.)

Karen?

KAREN

I'm tired.

STEVEN

You're mad.

KAREN

I'm cranky. There's a difference.

STEVEN

Either way you're kind of being a bitch.

        (Silence.)

KAREN

I think I may have feelings for you.

(Pause. STEVEN stays still for a moment, then slowly reaches over to turn the radio off.)

STEVEN

What?

KAREN

If I'm right … which I don't know if I am—but I think I could be, so I think I should let you know that there is a possibility that I—maybe, you know—like I'm … falling for you … like more than just a friend.

(Beat.)

I shouldn't have said that. It was inappropriate. I—I shouldn't have done that.

(Pause.)

STEVEN

(Still processing)

Why?

KAREN

I don't know. I mean, you're loud. You're obnoxious. You have a very odd smell. But for some reason, I can't ever stop thinking about you.

STEVEN

Karen …

KAREN

I know! I know. You don't have to say it.

STEVEN

We work together.

KAREN

Please don't.

STEVEN

There are rules.

KAREN

Stop! This is confusing so ... So just stop.

>  (Pause. THEY stare ahead. Silence. After a moment, STEVEN takes KAREN's hand.)

STEVEN

Hey, wake up.

>  (KAREN jumps realizing SHE was asleep. SHE sits upright, more awake and aware this time.)

KAREN

I'm up! Where are we?

STEVEN

Nowhere.

KAREN

Looks like vast areas of nothingness.

STEVEN

>  (Smiling at her)

I was just thinking that.

  KAREN

You and me.

                                              STEVEN

Great minds and all that?

                                                KAREN

Exactly.

      (The car rolls on.)

                                              STEVEN

Sleep well?

                                              KAREN

Not really.

      (Beat.)

I think we should stop for the night.

                                              STEVEN

Where?

                                              KAREN

We could stop here.

                                              STEVEN

      (Looks around)
Works for me.

      (THEY exit the interstate. Long pause.)

                        KAREN
Steven?

                        STEVEN
What's up?

                        KAREN
   (Beat)
Do you want the *Holiday Inn* or the *Motel 6*?

                        STEVEN
As long as it has a shower, I don't really care.

                        KAREN
Great ... Steven—?

                        STEVEN
Here we are.

      (THEY park. And sit. Silence.)

                        KAREN
You wanna get the room or unload the car?

                        STEVEN
Just one room?

                        KAREN
The company's not going to pay for two rooms. They wouldn't even pay to fly us
to the conference. And I'm not paying for one.

                        STEVEN
Neither am I.

KAREN

So what do you want?

STEVEN

I'll get the room.

KAREN

Great. Make sure you get a double.

(STEVEN exits the vehicle. The car transforms into the bed of the motel room. The lights shift. KAREN stirs and looks out over the audience.)

I sit in the driver's seat. Watching the road reveal itself to me as I travel along. All of the sudden, I'm no longer driving. I look to my left, towards the driver. But all I see is a shadow. A void. A nothingness … I should be afraid, but I'm not. I'm invigorated, because I'm on the road. I have a destination. A direction.

(Beat.)

I awake from this dream to find myself in another dream. I sit at a table. The table is … huge. As if four, maybe five of the largest conference tables you've ever seen have come together into one. One single, monstrous table. I can smell the table. It's made of pine. I can actually smell that distinct pine-tree smell. Like a mountain forest. I take my palm and caress the top of the table only to find that I've become stuck to the surface. The table is leaking sap. Oozing. Like sweat, and I'm stuck to it. You'd think that would upset me … It doesn't.

(SHE sits up in her seat. Beat.)

These dreams I keep waking up from … ? They're killing me.

(STEVEN enters, carrying two paper cups of coffee.)

                    STEVEN
Good morning.

                    KAREN
It's morning?

                    STEVEN
You slept all night.

                    KAREN
I don't even remember getting out of the car.

                    STEVEN
You didn't.

                    KAREN
How'd I get in here?

                    STEVEN
I carried you.

                    KAREN
How'd I get into bed?

                    STEVEN
I put you there.

                    KAREN
Everything's so ... fuzzy. Did I shower? Even brush my teeth?

                    STEVEN
You tried. I would have helped, but I was pretty sure you wouldn't have appreci-
ated me helping you take a shower.

                            KAREN

Thanks …

    (STEVEN sits next to her.)

What are you doing?

                            STEVEN

I'm sitting.

                            KAREN

Why?

                            STEVEN

'Cause I don't want to stand?

                            KAREN

Well don't.

    (SHE stands.)

We should get back on the road.

    (The scene shifts. Back in the car. KAREN is behind the wheel.)

Sure you don't want to drive?

                            STEVEN

Not yet. Maybe in a bit.

    (Beat.)

                              KAREN

The scenery is getting a lot prettier.


                              STEVEN

It's the mountains. Mountains are prettier.


                              KAREN

I was here when I was younger. Well, near here. I was camping with my family. One afternoon, we took a boat across the lake. It was gorgeous. Seeing the water. It would have been like glass except for the ripples from where the water was hitting the boat. And all I could hear was the wind. Just a gentle breeze. Nobody was talking. No sounds of a motor running. Just the wind. Which of course isn't true. My mind has completely manipulated that memory. There were at least twenty people on that boat, so there had to have been some talking. And the boat was huge, so there had to have been a motor, a loud one. But my brain doesn't remember that. Only the visuals. And the wind. Weird, huh? How your brain can just change the way you remember things?

> (SHE looks over to find STEVEN has fallen asleep. SHE smiles, reaches over and runs her hand through his hair. Her smile fades as SHE looks back to the road.)

We got to the other side of the lake, and my mom saw a sign saying that the camp ground was only a third of a mile away, so we decided to hike back. Turns out it was three miles away. And three miles is a long way for a seven-year-old. But we did it. All three miles.

> (Beat.)

We laugh about it now. Which is good. It's nice. Just to laugh about something so silly.

> (STEVEN jumps, startling himself awake.)

STEVEN

Holy hell, I just had the weirdest dream!


KAREN

Yeah?


STEVEN

Yeah. I was on the run. I broke out of jail, and ran away, and become, like this fugitive. Everyone was after me, and I didn't know what to do. But I had thirty-nine dollars, so I decided to go to the thrift store and buy some new clothes. And the people who worked there, they were so nice. They like, cooked me dinner. And talked to me about baseball. And why thirty-nine dollars? What's the significance of thirty-nine? Why not forty? Or thirty-five?


KAREN

How much cash do you have now?

(STEVEN frantically pulls out his wallet, and counts his cash.)

STEVEN

Thirty-nine dollars ... Whoa ...


KAREN

I think you're reading too much into it. Sometimes a dream is just a dream.


STEVEN

And sometimes it isn't.


KAREN

Sometimes it is.

STEVEN

Sometimes it's more. Like now. What if this means something more? What about the fugitive part? What if I'm unconsciously seeing into the future? What if I'm about to commit a crime, and I don't even know it?

KAREN

What were you in jail for?

STEVEN

I can't remember. Something minor, though. I knew that by escaping and running away, I was making things much worse than they needed to be. Like I wasn't helping myself out.

KAREN

Maybe that's the real message. To not make your problems any bigger than they have to be.

STEVEN

Right … You were in it. I saw you with some guy. You were kissing.

(Silence.)

KAREN

Was he cute?

STEVEN

Not really.

(Silence. THEY drive on.)

KAREN

Where'd you stay when you were here last year?

STEVEN

I wasn't here last year.

KAREN

You said you were.

STEVEN

No, I didn't.

KAREN

Yesterday, you said you went to last year's Omegatech Conference.

STEVEN

I have never heard of Omegatech. Are you all right?

KAREN

I must have dreamed it.

STEVEN

I wish I was here last year. This is gorgeous.

KAREN

It is.

STEVEN

Much prettier than on TV.

KAREN

Usually when they show the mountains on TV, it's filmed in California.

STEVEN

*Mork and Mindy.*

KAREN

What?

STEVEN

*Mork and Mindy*. It took place in Boulder, Colorado but was filmed in California.

KAREN

Random.

STEVEN

You brought it up.

(Looks out his window.)

Are the mountains getting bigger?

KAREN

Seems like it.

STEVEN

The higher we go, the taller they get. Like they're looking down on us or something.

KAREN

I think they're beautiful. Majestic.

STEVEN

Yeah, they're beautiful. I just hope we don't go driving off the side of one of 'em.

(KAREN looks out the window as SHE drives. A winged fish flies by smoking a cigarette.)

                              KAREN

Huh.


                              STEVEN

What?


                              KAREN

Nothing. A fish just flew by.


                              STEVEN

I didn't know flying fish were in this area of the country.


                              KAREN

I don't think they are.

       (Pause.)


                              STEVEN

You're awfully calm for having seen a fish fly in front of you.


                              KAREN

Past me.


                              STEVEN

What?


                              KAREN

Past me. He flew past me.


                              STEVEN

He?

KAREN

Sure, why not?

STEVEN

You're okay with the flying fish.

KAREN

I don't think I'm awake right now, so it doesn't really matter.

STEVEN

Oh ...

(Silence.)

If you're not awake, then who's driving the car?

KAREN

Nobody.

(HE's confused.)

We're not even here, Steven.

STEVEN

Then where are we?

KAREN

I just assumed that we're still back at the hotel. Or maybe I'm still at home, snuggled up in my own bed. Maybe I never even went on this trip.

STEVEN

Then what am I doing here?

KAREN

You're a part of my dream. This isn't that difficult Steven. Just accept it.

STEVEN

But I just had a dream. I had a dream that you couldn't have known about. You had no idea.

KAREN

Unless I created your dream as a part of my dream. Look, maybe this is your dream. But I've had several dreams already, which leads me to believe that you're the one in my head.

STEVEN

I don't think that's the case. I don't think you're dreaming. I wouldn't be this afraid for my life if you were dreaming.

KAREN

Afraid for your life?

STEVEN

If you're asleep, and I'm asleep, nobody's driving the car.

KAREN

If we're in the car at all.

STEVEN

We can't both be dreaming the same dream. We can't both be in the same dream.

KAREN

So, what, you're saying that this is your dream?

STEVEN

I'm saying that this isn't a dream.

KAREN

Don't be stupid, a fish just flew past us. Wings and everything. I think he was smoking a cigarette, too.

STEVEN

This is disturbing.

KAREN

Let's just pretend for a moment, that this is a dream, and we're both consciously aware of that.

STEVEN

I don't—

KAREN

I know imagination isn't one of your strong points, but give it a shot!

STEVEN

How?

KAREN

Say something. Say something that you wouldn't normally say if you were awake. See what happens.

(STEVEN turns and looks out, pondering.)

STEVEN

I have feelings for you. I don't know what the feelings mean. But I ... I feel. For you. I want you. I think about you all the time, and how you make me feel. It's invigorating and frustrating all at the same time. In the mornings, I can't wait

STEVEN (con't)
to go to work because I get to see you. I want to be with you so much that I imagine—I fantasize about us. About you and me sharing a life together.

(Beat.)

I'm sorry. I shouldn't have said anything. That was selfish.

(Long pause.)

Karen?

KAREN
I heard you.

STEVEN
And?

KAREN
I have feelings for you too.

STEVEN
Really?

KAREN
Don't ask me why?

STEVEN
I have to. Why do you like me? I'm loud. I'm extremely obnoxious at times. I, for some reason, seem to be permeating a smell, which is completely new to me.

KAREN
Yet, I can't stop thinking about you.

STEVEN

We're co-workers. There are rules.

KAREN

So I've heard.

(Silence.)

STEVEN

So is this my dream then?

KAREN

I guess.

(Beat.)

Maybe.

(Beat.)

I don't know, probably not.

STEVEN

Why?

KAREN

Because if this were your dream, you would be dreaming about having a dream, which occurred during a dream where you were dreaming about how I was dreaming that I wake up from a dream within a dream.

STEVEN

(Beat)
I think my brain just exploded.

                    KAREN
That happens when you think too hard.

                    STEVEN
My head hurts! The point is my head hurts!

                    KAREN
Don't get mad at me.

                    STEVEN
What the hell is going on?!

                    KAREN
Stop yelling! Just look out your window until you can control yourself.

    (STEVEN turns, pouting.)

                    KAREN
    (Under her breath)
Like a child …

                    STEVEN
You started it.

                    KAREN
Look out your window!

    (The thumping returns. There's more rhythm to it this time. A definite beat.
    THEY hear it and look at each other, quietly returning to their previous
    positions. THEY drive on.)

                    STEVEN
Karen?

KAREN

I'm not talking to you unless you've calmed down.

STEVEN

(Pointing out his window)
Do you see that?

KAREN

(Looking for a moment)
Buffalo.

STEVEN

Yeah, but they're ...

KAREN

They're dancing.

(THEY return to their positions.)

STEVEN

I don't think I dance as often as I should.

KAREN

That's kind of sad.

STEVEN

Yeah. It is.

(THEY drive on.)

KAREN

Look!

                          STEVEN
What?

                          KAREN
The lake. Wait for it. There.

                          STEVEN
Wow ...

                          KAREN
I'm pulling over.

                          STEVEN
Why?

                          KAREN
To look at it. Unless you want me to risk driving through the guardrail.

                          STEVEN
 ... pull over ...

        (SHE does. THEY stare out through the windshield.)

                          KAREN
        (Moving to exit the car)
I want a closer look.

                          STEVEN
Wait.

                          KAREN
What?

### STEVEN

What—what if this is just a dream? Mine, yours, it doesn't matter. If this has all been a dream, somebody must be trying to send us a message.

### KAREN

Does it matter?

### STEVEN

What's going to happen when we wake up?

### KAREN

Dreams are an experience. A journey into the unconscious parts of your mind. Just let it be what it is.

(Beat.)

### STEVEN

Once, I dreamed that I was a superhero. I had all these powers and could do all these things. But the city, my city, the one I was protecting, was completely empty. I had all these abilities and could do so much. But there was nobody around for me to help. It was awful. Lonely. All I wanted to do was make things better. Fly down and save people. Sweep everyone off their feet. Take them away to worlds of unknown potential and endless possibilities. What's wrong with that?

### KAREN

(Beat)
You could take me away? I mean, if you want. I like you, and you like me, right? So why not?

### STEVEN

I'll most likely end up ruining everything.

KAREN

I'm scared, too.

(A distant melody plays ... somewhere.)

You hear that?

STEVEN

Music.

KAREN

I think you should dance with me.

STEVEN

We'd have to get out of the car.

KAREN

That should be a fairly easy thing to do.

STEVEN

I'm not a very good dancer.

KAREN

If the buffalo can dance, so can you.

(SHE reaches out and takes his hand.)

STEVEN

I'd love to.

(THEY look back out at the lake.)

                              KAREN

It really is beautiful.

                              STEVEN

Like a dream come true.

        (THEY begin to smile. STEVEN abruptly wakes up. KAREN is driving and
        has been for quite some time.)

                              KAREN

Good! You're awake.

        (Lights fade.)


                          **END OF PLAY**

# For Further Consideration: An Exercise on Analysis

1. What are three elements of Surrealism that have influenced this play (you may need to do some further research)?
2. If this play has elements of comedy as suggested, then what are three fundamentals of comedy at work in dREAMtRIPPIN' (you may need to do some further research)?
3. Identify three ways that the form of the script indicates that this is a hybrid play.
4. What are the given circumstances of the play as found in the Cast of Characters list and the stage directions?
5. Now that you have finished reading the play, what do you want to know more about exactly?

# For Further Research

Breton, André. *What Is Surrealism?: Selected Writings.* Edited by Franklin Rosemont. New York: Pathfinder Press, 1978.

Kaplan, Steve. *The Hidden Tools of Comedy: The Serious Business of Being Funny.* Studio City, CA: Michael Wiese Productions, 2013.

Klingsöhr-Leroy, Cathrin. *Surrealism.* Cologne, Germany: Taschen, 2015.

Polizzotti, Mark. *Revolution of the Mind: The Life of André Breton.* Boston: Black Widow Press, 2009.

Wortheim, Arthur Frank. *W. C. Fields from Burlesque and Vaudeville to Broadway: Becoming a Comedian.* New York: Palgrave Macmillan, 2014.

# CHAPTER 4

# Kiri Palm

PLAYWRIGHT

## *UNSER ZUVERLÄSSIGES HAUS*

©2009 Kiri Palm

### PRODUCTION HISTORY

UNSER ZUVERLÄSSIGES HAUS was first seen in 2010 at the Journeys Short Play Festival. In 2011 it was a featured performance at the Kennedy Center American College Theatre Festival, Region III gathering in East Lansing, Michigan, directed by Callie Meiners who directed it again for the Minnesota Fringe Festival in 2017 under the title "A Dream Deferred." Core Project Chicago's Going Dutch Festival also produced the play in 2013.

### CAST OF CHARACTERS
    YOUNG WOMAN
    HEAD OF HOUSING
    EMPLOYEES
    SECRETARY
    GUARD

YOUNG MAN

SETTING—The Housing Office of Pyrite Point. Three o'clock and then later.

**PLAYWRIGHT'S NOTE**

This play can use as few as four actors if desired. The male characters can be double-cast as the following:

MAN 1
HEAD OF HOUSING
YOUNG MAN

MAN 2
EMPLOYEES
GUARD

# About the Playwright

Kiri Palm's other plays include *Table Settings* and *Fairies.* Her work has been produced at Good Acting Studio (Marietta, Georgia), Strangeloop Theatre (Chicago), Core Project Chicago, and Southern Illinois University (SIU). Kiri holds BA degrees in Theatre and in German Studies from SIU. She lives in Chicago.

# Form and Style

The rough English translation of the title is "Our Reliable House," and in this play we see a mild-mannered college student entering the rather unique world of college housing. The play is inspired by the form and style of both Expressionism and Theater of the Absurd, and it quickly draws us into what happens as our main character, Young Woman, goes about trying to find a home. Both she and we encounter a world that is out of harmony and (only slightly) disjointed.

As Expressionism found its way from the visual arts of the early twentieth century into theatre and live performance, practitioners were interested in exploring techniques that rebelled against those of Theatrical Realism. One of the key ways writers do this is by focusing on the inner psychology of a particular character. This means that the world of the play is shaped by how the character perceives the world. Additionally, key to writing any piece of Expressionism is dramatizing the nightmarish state of the human condition, so the atmosphere of many plays of this type was a bit eerie and slightly carnivalesque. These plays usually have distortions in setting, use few props, and often have main characters with names that indicate their state of mind or the character's function (for example, Young Woman). These characters often speak in clipped phrases that stand in juxtaposition to long pauses and monologues. As for content, taboo topics (in the case of our play, the inner workings of the student housing enterprise on college and university campuses) are more often than not the subject of Expressionist plays. In this case, Palm borrows inspiration for her first scene from Sophie Treadwell's *Machinal*.

**Theatre of the Absurd**, also called **Absurdism**, is a form and a style that focuses on the irrationality and illogicality of the human condition. Another way to think about it is that Theatre of the Absurd is concerned with a world that is devoid of reason. It has nothing to do with being bizarre, what we might think of as "absurd" in the vernacular sense. Apparently, the advent and use of nuclear weapons during World War II pushed some writers—like Samuel Beckett, Eugene Ionesco, and Jean Genet—to pause and consider how fragile our world truly is. These writers were masters at using meaningless and repetitious dialogue, confusing situations, and incoherent human relations to drive home a point. The atmosphere of these plays often begins as subdued and sober—before bursting into a comical succession, only to return to subdued and sober. Most interesting, perhaps, is the way that writers of Absurdism highlight the use of language as an ineffective communication tool. Look for this in Palm's play.

# Plays for Further Study

There are several great examples of Expressionism in American theatre and drama. *The Adding Machine* by Elmer Rice is one that always tops our list. Seemingly inspired by Rice's trip to see the Ford assembly line in action, this play follows Mr. Zero, an accountant at a large corporation for over twenty years, and his eventual replacement by an automated adding machine. *Bury the Dead* by Irwin Shaw dramatizes the refusal of dead soldiers from an unnamed conflict to be buried. In fact, they plead to rejoin the land of the living. Each comes from the grave to discuss the futility of war, among other topics—to no avail. Subtitled "A Jazz Symphony of American Life in Four Acts," John Howard Lawson's *Processional* recounts the hardships and misadventures of a coal strike leader in a West Virginia town. For those who might be interested in seeing how early twentieth-century Expressionism looks on film, we recommend watching *The Cabinet of Dr. Caligari, The Golem, Metropolis*, or *Nosferatu*.

Theatre of the Absurd has several fine examples to choose from for getting acquainted with the form. *Waiting for Godot,* by Samuel Beckett, is perhaps one of the best-known plays of this genre. The characters Estragon and Vladimir are carrying on a conversation near a tree as they wait for the arrival of a man named Godot. As they go about their waiting, Lucky and Pozzo come by the tree. Eventually they leave, with Estragon and Vladimir still waiting for Godot. All the characters seem to be struggling with a world without an inherent understanding of truth. Eugene Ionesco's *The Bald Soprano* is a longer one-act play that focuses on the Smiths. The world of this play is one where the clock indicates the opposite of the actual time and where Mr. and Mrs. Smith spend a good amount of time deducing that they live in the same house and sleep in the same bed (this scene is somewhat famous in theatre history for what it does and how it does it). *The Balcony,* by Jean Genet, is set in the House of Illusions, also known as The Grand Balcony. This is a place where men, largely, come to live out fantasies. The play points out how the cliché "Be careful what you wish for" really does carry weight.

## CAUTION

# UNSER ZUVERLÄSSIGES HAUS

CAST OF CHARACTERS
> YOUNG WOMAN—A student attempting to find a home
> HEAD OF HOUSING—Lord and master of residency
> EMPLOYEES—A busy group of clowns
> SECRETARY—Immediate underling, well-dressed
> GUARD—Protector of the lord and master
> YOUNG MAN—A student with good intentions in mind

SETTING—The Housing Office of Pyrite Point. Three o'clock and then later.

**AT RISE:** The Main Lobby has a large desk with three telephones atop it, filing cabinets towering against the walls, and a low-sitting chair. There are three doors: one leading to the outside world, another leading to the Head of Housing's Throne Room, the third leading to a storage room resplendent with dimestore treasures. The Throne Room, adjacent on the stage to the main lobby, is large, luxurious, and heavily guarded.

A SECRETARY sits at the desk, answering the constantly ringing telephones with robotic accuracy. The HEAD OF HOUSING sits in his throne in the adjacent room, eating a bowl of grapes. EMPLOYEES, dressed as clowns and circus performers, enter and exit from the doors leading to the storage room and corridor at mechanical intervals

> throughout the play, carrying heavy
> boxes laden with carnival goods. This
> is a place of chaos.

SECRETARY

Housing office! Please hold. Housing office! Please hold! Mr. J. isn't here right now, may I take a message? Mr. J. isn't here right now, may I ask who's calling?

EMPLOYEE 1

(Crossing from storage room to corridor)
Hot dogs! Comin' through!

SECRETARY

We don't offer specialized rooms, thank you for calling. We don't offer specialized rooms, thank you for calling.

EMPLOYEE 2

(Crossing from storage room to corridor)
Cotton candy!

SECRETARY

Housing office! Please hold. Housing office! Please hold.

EMPLOYEE 3

(Crossing from storage room to corridor)
Candy apples! Hold the door!

SECRETARY

Mr. J. isn't here right now, may I take a message?

HEAD OF HOUSING

(From the throne room)
Ka-tie!

SECRETARY

Co-ming!

(SHE rises with a stenography pad and struts into the throne room. A YOUNG WOMAN enters. SHE closes the door behind her and looks about the surrounding.)

EMPLOYEE 1
(Crossing from corridor to storage room)
Rubber ducks!

(YOUNG WOMAN narrowly dodges him. EMPLOYEE sees her enter. THEY are alone. The phone rings.)

Ahem.

(EMPLOYEE crosses to phone and answers it as SECRETARY. The following lines continue as long as the SECRETARY remains offstage.

Housing office! Please hold. Housing office! Please hold.

Mr. J isn't here right now, may I take a message?

Mr. J isn't in right now, may I ask who's calling?

We don't offer specialized rooms, thank you for calling.

We don't offer specialized rooms, thank you for calling.

(SECRETARY enters from throne room and heads to her desk, snatching the phone from EMPLOYEE. EMPLOYEE exits.)

SECRETARY

Housing office! Please hold. Housing office! Please hold.

EMPLOYEE 2

(Crossing from corridor to storage room)

Croutons!

(YOUNG WOMAN crosses to SECRETARY'S desk.)

YOUNG WOMAN

Uhm, excuse me ...

SECRETARY

(Holding up a finger)

Housing office! Please hold.

EMPLOYEE 3

(Crossing from corridor to storage room)

Balloon animals!

SECRETARY

(Pointing to the small chair)

Housing office! Please hold.

YOUNG WOMAN

(Backing up towards chair)

O ... kay.

(SHE sits.)

SECRETARY

Mr. J. isn't in right now, may I ask who's calling?

SECRETARY (con't)
We don't offer specialized rooms, thank you for calling.

We don't offer specialized rooms, thank you for calling.

(To YOUNG WOMAN.)

What?

What?

YOUNG WOMAN
Oh! Yes. Hello.

SECRETARY
What?

YOUNG WOMAN
I'd like to speak to the head of housing, if I could.

SECRETARY
Mr. J. isn't in right now.

YOUNG WOMAN
Yes. I know. But it's terribly important.

SECRETARY
We don't offer specialized rooms.

YOUNG WOMAN
Yes, I know about that. That's not why I need to speak to him.

SECRETARY

May I take a message?

YOUNG WOMAN

I'd rather speak to him personally, if it's all the same.

SECRETARY

No one speaks to Mr. J. No one but us.

YOUNG WOMAN

Perhaps he could make an exception.

SECRETARY

I can take a message.

YOUNG WOMAN

He said I had to talk to him.

EMPLOYEE 1
     (Crossing from storage room to corridor)
Hot sauce!

SECRETARY

Why would he talk to you? No one speaks to Mr. J. No one but us.

YOUNG WOMAN

He sent me a message. That's all it said.

(Removing a piece of paper from her purse and reading it aloud.)

"Ms. Mann, I am very interested in your problem. Please come to the housing office tomorrow afternoon at three o'clock to discuss it further with me. Sincerely, Mr. J."

SECRETARY
I didn't send out that letter. Guard!

EMPLOYEE 2
(Crossing from storage room to corridor)
Elephant ears!

YOUNG WOMAN
Wait! You can't just throw me out!

SECRETARY
Can and will!

YOUNG WOMAN
But he told me to come see him!

SECRETARY
Nonsense! Hogwash!

EMPLOYEE 3
(Crossing from storage room to corridor)
Baloney!

SECRETARY
This is the silliest stuff that ever I heard!

YOUNG WOMAN
But Mr. J.—!

SECRETARY
Guard!

(A GUARD enters and apprehends the YOUNG WOMAN.)

                    HEAD OF HOUSING
     (Calling from adjacent room)
Ka-tie!

                       SECRETARY
Co-ming!

     (All action in the office halts as SHE skips into the throne room once more.
     YOUNG WOMAN is suspended from the arms of the GUARD. Whispering.)

She's here!

                    HEAD OF HOUSING
     (Whispering)
She's here?

                       SECRETARY
     (Whispering)
Right outside.

                    HEAD OF HOUSING
     (Whispering)
Oh, yes!

     (THEY kiss passionately.)

                     YOUNG WOMAN
     (To GUARD)
Uh ... hi.

GUARD

Ah-hem.

SECRETARY

    (Prompting)
She wants to see you.

HEAD OF HOUSING

WHAT DO YOU MEAN, "SOMEONE WANTS TO SEE ME"?

    (THEY kiss.)

YOUNG WOMAN

    (To GUARD)
Do … do you think you could put me down?

GUARD

Ah-*hem*.

SECRETARY

She's even more unaware than we thought.

HEAD OF HOUSING

Completely oblivious?

SECRETARY

Airhead!

    (HEAD OF HOUSING kisses up SECRETARY'S leg.)

YOUNG WOMAN

I can't feel my hands.

GUARD

Ah-hem!

HEAD OF HOUSING

(Between kisses)
NO ONE IS ALLOWED TO SEE ME! NOT NOBODY, NOT NO-HOW!

YOUNG WOMAN

Or … my feet.

SECRETARY

Oh! Your kisses are like starlight!

HEAD OF HOUSING

And yours are candy! Like cherry cordials!

(SECRETARY rips open her bustier.)

OH, WHAT?? "MS. MANN"? WHAT KIND OF NAME IS THAT? You foxy—

(THEY kiss. Fireworks are heard in the distance. GUARD pulls a box of Tic Tacs out of his pocket. HE offers them to YOUNG WOMAN.)

YOUNG WOMAN

Oh! Thank you.

SECRETARY

Shall I send her to you?

HEAD OF HOUSING

Shall I send you to my boudoir?

SECRETARY

Shall I wear my chasuble?

HEAD OF HOUSING

With fishnets.

SECRETARY

I went to Frederick's yesterday.

HEAD OF HOUSING

(Moaning)
A MESSAGE YOU SAY? FINE. Oh yes, you are so fine. SEND HER IN.

(THEIR passion ignites the stage. GUARD and YOUNG WOMAN munch complacently. HEAD OF HOUSING and SECRETARY part dramatically. BOTH fumble with their disheveled clothes. SECRETARY enters main room.)

SECRETARY

Mr. J. will see you now.

(The GUARD drops her.)

YOUNG WOMAN

Oof!

SECRETARY

Right away! Don't delay!

YOUNG WOMAN

Okay, okay. I'm going.

(YOUNG WOMAN is escorted into the Throne Room by the GUARD and SECRETARY. The HEAD OF HOUSING is surrounded by majesty.)

HEAD OF HOUSING

You! Who are you? Who sent you? Why are you here??

YOUNG WOMAN

Sheila Mann, sir. I called your office two weeks ago. You sent me a message yesterday.

HEAD OF HOUSING

Message? What kind of message?

YOUNG WOMAN

I have it right here, sir.

(Removing the piece of paper as before.)

"Ms. Mann, I am very interested in your problem. Please come to the housing office tomorrow afternoon at three o'clock to discuss it further with me. Sincerely, Mr. J."

HEAD OF HOUSING

Let me see that!

(HE snaps his fingers. The SECRETARY struts to YOUNG WOMAN, takes the letter, and takes it to HEAD OF HOUSING.)

Hm. Hm. Yes, that does seem to be something I would write. Where did you get this?

YOUNG WOMAN

You sent it to me, sir.

HEAD OF HOUSING

Yes, yes. Why did I send it to you?

YOUNG WOMAN
Well, sir, I assumed—

SECRETARY and GUARD
When you assume, you make an ass of you and me!

YOUNG WOMAN
(Confused)
I assumed it had something to do with my new room.

SECRETARY
We don't offer specialized rooms!

YOUNG WOMAN
I've … been having roommate issues.

HEAD OF HOUSING
Issues? What kind of issues?

YOUNG WOMAN
We haven't been getting along very well.

HEAD OF HOUSING
Does she smoke crack?

YOUNG WOMAN
No …

HEAD OF HOUSING
Has she threatened you physically?

YOUNG WOMAN
Not exactly …

HEAD OF HOUSING

NO ISSUE!

YOUNG WOMAN

If you'll just listen to me—

HEAD OF HOUSING

NO TIME! NO TIME! THINGS TO DO! VERY BUSY!

(HE snaps his fingers. The GUARD begins to remove YOUNG WOMAN.)

YOUNG WOMAN

She's damaged my belongings!

HEAD OF HOUSING

How so?

YOUNG WOMAN

She set my mattress on fire.

HEAD OF HOUSING

So?

YOUNG WOMAN

"So"? What do you mean "so"? My mattress was on fire!

HEAD OF HOUSING

Were you on the mattress at the time?

YOUNG WOMAN

No—

                                        HEAD OF HOUSING
NO TIME! NO TIME!

                                        YOUNG WOMAN
She threatened me!

                                        HEAD OF HOUSING
Did she threaten your life?

                                        YOUNG WOMAN
Well—

                                        HEAD OF HOUSING
Was there a knife to your throat?

                                        YOUNG WOMAN
No—

                                        HEAD OF HOUSING
A gun to your head?

                                        YOUNG WOMAN
Not really …

                                        HEAD OF HOUSING
NOT GOOD ENOUGH.

                                        YOUNG WOMAN
She … called me a kike!

                                        HEAD OF HOUSING
Did she call you a heeb?

YOUNG WOMAN

What? No!

HEAD OF HOUSING

THERE'S NOTHING WE CAN DO. Take her!

YOUNG WOMAN

Wait! Wait! Okay. Fine.

She ...

She tried to have sex with me.

HEAD OF HOUSING

Ridiculous!

YOUNG WOMAN

She did! She touched me sexually!

HEAD OF HOUSING

Liar! Wouldn't your mother be ashamed!

YOUNG WOMAN

Why would I lie about this?

HEAD OF HOUSING

Excuses! Mindless excuses! Guard!

YOUNG WOMAN

She touched me sexually! I swear it's true!

HEAD OF HOUSING

Are you in love with her?

YOUNG WOMAN

What?

HEAD OF HOUSING

You two could be very happy together.

YOUNG WOMAN

She's my roommate.

SECRETARY and GUARD

Absence makes the heart grow fonder!

YOUNG WOMAN

What absence?

HEAD OF HOUSING

It would be easy to ask her to move in with you.

YOUNG WOMAN

She has a boyfriend!

HEAD OF HOUSING

She simply sounds confused. She could probably use a friend.

YOUNG WOMAN

Are you even listening to me?

HEAD OF HOUSING

She could probably use your comfort.

YOUNG WOMAN

Do you speak English?

HEAD OF HOUSING

And you're not giving it to her.

YOUNG WOMAN

Hello?

HEAD OF HOUSING

YOU ARE A BAD FRIEND!

SECRETARY and GUARD

Haste makes waste!

YOUNG WOMAN

That doesn't even make sense ...

HEAD OF HOUSING

We don't help lay-abouts.

YOUNG WOMAN

Lay-abouts? I'm not a lay-about!

HEAD OF HOUSING

Well you look like one to me.

YOUNG WOMAN

I'm a scholarship student! I have a four-point-o! I volunteer at nursing homes!

HEAD OF HOUSING

I can't hear you when you're mumbling.

YOUNG WOMAN

My roommate is putting me in danger; she's throwing out racial slurs like they're parade candy; she's even molesting me! Don't you see how awful this is?

                        HEAD OF HOUSING
I've lost interest.

                        YOUNG WOMAN
Is this what you get paid for?

                        HEAD OF HOUSING
I don't get paid; I get compensated.

                        YOUNG WOMAN
For what?

                        HEAD OF HOUSING
For listening to lay-abouts like you.

        (HE blows a raspberry. SECRETARY giggles.)

                        YOUNG WOMAN
You don't seem to understand how important this is.

                        HEAD OF HOUSING
Unimportant! Immaterial! Impertinent!

                        YOUNG WOMAN
She's abusing me! Can't you see that?

                        HEAD OF HOUSING
Noise, noise. Silly, silly noise.

                        YOUNG WOMAN
I'm frightened of her!

        (HEAD OF HOUSING blows another raspberry. SHE is about to cry.)

YOUNG WOMAN (con't)
I just want to get away from her, okay? I just want to move out.

HEAD OF HOUSING
Always whine whine whine.

SECRETARY and GUARD
Would you like some cheese with your whine?

HEAD OF HOUSING
Prattling on about unimportant things …

YOUNG WOMAN
This is my life!

HEAD OF HOUSING
Well, you should've thought of that in the first place.

YOUNG WOMAN
I have to move out! I *have* to!

HEAD OF HOUSING
And *I* have to pay taxes. What a shame! What's the time?

YOUNG WOMAN
What?

HEAD OF HOUSING
What's the time, you silly girl?

YOUNG WOMAN
It's a quarter after three.

HEAD OF HOUSING

I must be going. Busy day!

YOUNG WOMAN

What?

HEAD OF HOUSING

Things to do. People to see. It is my lunch break, after all.

YOUNG WOMAN

Wait!

HEAD OF HOUSING

Good day!

YOUNG WOMAN

I'll go to the Dean for permission!

HEAD OF HOUSING

How ridiculous!

YOUNG WOMAN

Do you want money? I'll pay you!

HEAD OF HOUSING

How unethical!

YOUNG WOMAN

I'll take it to the courts!

HEAD OF HOUSING

You're too dramatic for my time. TTFN!

SECRETARY and GUARD

Ta-ta for now!

YOUNG WOMAN

Wait! Don't leave! I'll do anything you want!

HEAD OF HOUSING

Hmm?

YOUNG WOMAN

Please. Anything. Just help me.

HEAD OF HOUSING

Anything, you say?

YOUNG WOMAN

Anything.

SECRETARY and GUARD

Anything and everything?

YOUNG WOMAN

Yes! Anything and everything.

HEAD OF HOUSING

Words are like children, you know.

YOUNG WOMAN

I don't care! Just help me. Please.

                          HEAD OF HOUSING
Well.

Well, isn't that something?

Well, my dear. That *is* something.

          (HE snaps his fingers. The SECRETARY brings over a large scroll and quill.
          SHE unfurls it with a flick of her wrist.)

Sign here.

                          YOUNG WOMAN
What is it?

                          HEAD OF HOUSING
No questions, please, just sign.

                          YOUNG WOMAN
And this will help me?

                          HEAD OF HOUSING
You said you'd do anything.

                    SECRETARY and GUARD
Anything and everything.

                          HEAD OF HOUSING
So sign.

                          YOUNG WOMAN
On the dotted line?

                    HEAD OF HOUSING
On the dotted line.

                     YOUNG WOMAN
        (Studying quill)
There isn't any ink.

                    HEAD OF HOUSING
Oh, you won't need ink.

                     YOUNG WOMAN
And you're sure this will help me?

                    HEAD OF HOUSING
Just sign.

        (SHE begins to sign the scroll. The pain is instantaneous. SHE flinches
        away.)

Anything and everything.

        (YOUNG WOMAN strengthens her resolve and signs. Her name shines
        bright and red: blood. The SECRETARY whisks the scroll and quill away and
        exits.)

Well! That ought to do it!

                     YOUNG WOMAN
        (Weakly)
Do what?

                    HEAD OF HOUSING
I think we can find someplace for you now. Ka-tie!

> SECRETARY
> (From lobby)
Co-ming!

> YOUNG WOMAN
Really?

> HEAD OF HOUSING
No questions, please.

> SECRETARY
> (Entering)
Yes, Mr. J.

> HEAD OF HOUSING
Take Ms. Mann to our specialized rooms, please.

> YOUNG WOMAN
Specialized?

> SECRETARY
Yes, Mr. J.

> YOUNG WOMAN
But you don't offer specialized rooms.

> HEAD OF HOUSING
Well, not to *everyone*.

> SECRETARY
Of course not!

                    SECRETARY and GUARD
You're not special if everyone's special.

                        YOUNG WOMAN
I don't understand.

                      HEAD OF HOUSING
You think too much.

                    SECRETARY and GUARD
Much too much.

                      HEAD OF HOUSING
*I* don't think.

                         SECRETARY
Nor I!

                           GUARD
Nor I!

                        YOUNG WOMAN
This is getting creepy.

                         SECRETARY
Let's take you to your specialized room.

                      HEAD OF HOUSING
Don't make her mad, girl.

                        YOUNG WOMAN
Mad?

HEAD OF HOUSING

I'm mad. *You're* mad …

SECRETARY and GUARD

We're all mad here!

YOUNG WOMAN

I think I'd like to go home now.

HEAD OF HOUSING

Oh, you can't go home.

YOUNG WOMAN

No, really, I appreciate this and all, but now that I think of it, my roommate and I can handle our problems on our own.

HEAD OF HOUSING

I don't think you understand.

SECRETARY

Guard!

HEAD OF HOUSING

You can't. Go. Home.

(GUARD seizes YOUNG WOMAN.)

YOUNG WOMAN

(Screaming)
HELP!

SECRETARY

Quiet now: there's no need to get excited.

HEAD OF HOUSING

No one can hear you, my dear.

GUARD

(In agreement)
Ah-HEM!

YOUNG WOMAN

Let me GO!

HEAD OF HOUSING

You don't want that.

YOUNG WOMAN

This is kidnapping!

SECRETARY and GUARD

Kidnapping requires a kid.

YOUNG WOMAN

SHUT UP!

HEAD OF HOUSING

You're much too excited, my dear. Perhaps you'd like to go lay down.

(HE snaps his fingers. GUARDS begin to carry her off stage.)

YOUNG WOMAN

LET GO OF ME!

(Change. The YOUNG WOMAN breaks away. ALL OTHERS freeze onstage.)

Words are like children; they will run away if you let them.

YOUNG WOMAN (con't)

Get into trouble
Suffer
Die
We speak like fools and damn ourselves
We run
flee
race blindly
It's not our fault
not our fault
our fault

(HEAD OF HOUSING, SECRETARY and GUARD begin to whisper behind her. Their later quotes may be staggered as the director desires.)

| YOUNG WOMAN | ALL OTHERS |
|---|---|
| The pace has changed | Sheila Mann |
| the drive | |
| sudden discontent | |
| Out of the clouds comes damnation | Sheila Mann |
| I didn't know | |
| I was so young. I was | |
| unaware. | Sheila Mann |
| We wrestle & wrangle without care | |
| We run & separate & | |
| reduce. | Sheila Mann |
| We are told we are special and yet all the same. | |
| We are different in our similarity. | Sheila Mann |
| I didn't know | |

YO. WO.
I didn't know.
And had I
known? Would I
have
come into this
place? Probably.
And why?
Because I am no
better no worse.
There's nothing
wrong with
desiring
happiness.
One must only
know that there
are wolves.

GUARD
The higher
nature of the
great man
lies in being
different, in
incommuni-
cability, in
distance of
rank, not in
any effect
of any kind.

H. of H.
I am he that
liveth and was
dead,
and behold,
I am alive
forevermore
And have the
keys of hell
and of death.
(Repeat.)

Secr.
Wir gehen durch
die Kniechenhohl'.
Rennt, Alice, rennt.
Wir haben nur ein
bisschen Zeit.
Rennt, Alice, rennt.
(Repeat.)

Sheila Mann.

GUARD

YOUNG WOMAN
They will tear out your throat
they will devour your soul
They are your doom.
NO. No WE are our doom
our ending our hell.

GUARD
The higher nature of the great man lies
in being different, in incommunicability,
in distance of rank, not in any effect of
any kind.

Sheila Mann.

SECRETARY

YOUNG WOMAN
We go to the slaughter like
sheep! Easy targets for easy
consummation.

SECRETARY
Wir gehen durch die Kniechenhohl'.
Rennt, Alice, rennt. Wir haben nur
ein bisschen Zeit. Rennt, Alice, rennt.

                    HEAD OF HOUSING
Sheila Mann.

                    YOUNG WOMAN
I didn't know.

                    HEAD OF HOUSING
I am he that liveth and was dead and behold I am alive forevermore and have
the keys of hell and of death.

                    YOUNG WOMAN
I didn't know.

        (The action returns. The HEAD OF HOUSING stares pointedly at the now-
        mad YOUNG WOMAN.)

                    HEAD OF HOUSING
There's no need to get upset. After all,

                        ALL
This is what you wanted.

        (The GUARD begins to carry YOUNG WOMAN offstage. HEAD OF HOUSING
        and SECRETARY watch THEM impassively.)

                    YOUNG WOMAN
Let me go! Let me GO!

        (BLACKOUT.)

        (A moment.)

        (Another.)

(Lights rise on the lobby of the Pyrite Point Housing Office. Same as before, but a desk has been added with phones and a chair. Chaos.)

SECRETARY

Housing office! Please hold. Housing office! Please hold!

Mr. J. isn't here right now, may I take a message?

Mr. J. isn't here right now, may I ask who's calling?

EMPLOYEE 1
(Crossing from storage room to corridor)
Hot dogs! Comin' through!

SECRETARY

We don't offer specialized rooms, thank you for calling. We don't offer specialized rooms, thank you for calling.

EMPLOYEE 2
(Crossing from storage room to corridor)
Cotton candy!

SECRETARY

Housing office! Please hold. Housing office! Please hold.

EMPLOYEE 3
(Crossing from storage room to corridor)
Candy apples! Hold the door!

SECRETARY

Mr. J. isn't here right now, may I take a message?

HEAD OF HOUSING
(From the throne room)
Ka-tie!

SECRETARY

Co-ming!

(SHE rises swiftly with a stenography pad and struts into the throne room. As the SECRETARY crosses into the Throne Room, SHE is passed by the YOUNG WOMAN, also carrying a stenography pad and dressed as a secretary. Her movements are robotic and mechanized. SHE takes her seat behind the second desk.)

EMPLOYEE 1
(Crossing from corridor to storage room)
Rubber ducks!

YOUNG WOMAN
Housing office! Please hold. Housing office! Please hold.

Mr. J. isn't in right now, may I take a message?

We don't offer specialized rooms, thank you for calling.

EMPLOYEE 2
(Crossing from corridor to storage room)
Croutons!

YOUNG WOMAN
Housing office! Please hold. Housing office! Please hold.

Mr. J. isn't here right now, may I ask who's calling?

EMPLOYEE 3
(Crossing from corridor to storage room)
Balloon animals!

(A YOUNG MAN enters behind EMPLOYEE 3. HE closes the door behind him and looks about quizzically.)

YOUNG WOMAN
We don't offer specialized rooms, thank you for calling.

Housing office! Please hold. Housing office! Please hold.

Mr. J. isn't in right now, may I take a message?

EMPLOYEE 1
(Crossing from storage room to corridor)
Hot sauce!

(YOUNG MAN narrowly dodges him. EMPLOYEE sees him enter. EMPLOYEE exits into throne room.)

YOUNG WOMAN
We don't offer specialized rooms, thank you for calling. We don't offer specialized rooms, thank you for calling.

(YOUNG MAN crosses to YOUNG WOMAN'S desk.)

YOUNG MAN
Uhm, excuse me …

(SHE holds her finger up. Lights fade.)

**END OF PLAY**

# Group Playwriting: An Exercise on Absurdism

1. Break into teams of at least four, no more than six.
2. Randomly choose an object you have in your bag or on your person.
3. Place it in front of the person to your left.
4. Each person picks up the object in front of them, gives it a name that is opposite of what it is, and uses it in a way it is not intended to be used ... within reason.
5. Choose one object. Use the one that the group feels is most comical.
6. Write down the object's name, it's "unintended" use, and any discussion around the process of coming up with the name and the use.
7. Now using the selected object and selected use, repeat the process.
8. Create a short scene out of these two sequences. Discuss what you have. Does it need some linking dialog? Stage directions? To what extent does your scene reinforce the meaninglessness of words as communication tools?

# For Further Research

Bennett, Michael Y. *The Cambridge Introduction to Theatre and Literature of the Absurd.* Cambridge, UK: Cambridge University Press, 2015.

Berghaus, Günter. *Theatre, Performance, and the Historical Avant-Garde.* New York: Palgrave MacMillan, 2005.

Chambers, Jonathan L. *Messiah of the New Technique: John Howard Lawson, Communism, and American Theatre, 1923–1937.* Carbondale: Southern Illinois University Press, 2006.

Esslin, Martin. *The Theatre of the Absurd.* 3rd ed. New York: Vintage Books, 2001.

Walker, Julia A. *Expressionism and Modernism in the American Theatre: Bodies, Voices, Words.* Cambridge, UK: Cambridge University Press, 2005.

# CHAPTER 5

# Greg Aldrich

PLAYWRIGHT

## *THOUGHTS ON FLOOD PREVENTION*

©2015 Greg Aldrich

### PRODUCTION HISTORY

"Thoughts on Flood Prevention" premiered as a solo-performance monologue as part of Southern Illinois University's Big Muddy Shorts, the playwriting program's monthly festival for the performance of original short plays. It was revised and performed in the version that appears here in the Kleinau Theater Spotlight series, Department of Communication Studies, Southern Illinois University, Spring 2016.

### CAST OF CHARACTERS
    GREG

    SETTING—The theatre, now.

# About the Playwright

Originally from Alaska, Greg Aldrich received his BA from Benedictine College in Atchison, Kansas, and his MFA in Playwriting from Ohio University. He is currently completing his PhD at Southern Illinois University. Focused on the art and craft of adaptation, Greg's latest work has been on Fyodor Dostoyevsky—namely, a four-act adaptation entitled *Reflections on an Idiot*, based on *The Idiot*. Aldrich's full-length play *Epulosia* was a finalist for the Princess Grace Award in 2010. His other plays include *Beheading Vampire Puppies, The Moment After, Attack of the Ladybugs and the War That Wasn't, Typing Lear, The Body Snatcher, Looking Long into the Abyss,* and *The Principle of the Thing*. Aldrich states that he "writes about doubt" and that his plays explore "characters whose perceived order of the universe is thrown into sudden, uncomfortable doubt." He seeks to "explore the doubt that plagues us all ... ". Additionally, Aldrich is an environmental activist and has worked in the Office of Sustainability.

# Form and Style

Greg Aldrich takes as his form the solo-monologue, in the manner of Spalding Gray (to whom he alludes in the stage directions of "Thoughts on Flood Prevention"), Eric Bogosian, and others. Solo performers often practice **autoethnography**; that is, they research their own lives to provide inspiration or background for their works. In performance studies, artists/scholars expose their research methodology and speak directly to it. In Aldrich's short piece, for example, he mentions how he was recently exploring identity construction and masculinity in his doctoral program and how his studies led him to reflect on his father's view of what it means to be a man.

Performance Studies live events are intended to propel artists/scholars toward further research—and, as a result, to future performance. The solo pieces that these writers craft are often intensely personal, self-reflective, and revealing. Many include subject matter that some might consider "too much information" with regard to their creators' anxieties, sex lives, or participation in illicit activities. Rarely, then, are they performed by actors other than their authors (Eric Bogosian being an exception in some cases). While Aldrich incorporates incidents from his own life in "Thoughts on Flood Prevention," he does not over analyze or psychoanalyze the events used. Rather, he uses the flood metaphor—a real, physical, environmental threat—and his father's work as a hydrologist to explore the potential "flood of tears" we all anticipate with dread, hoping it does not strike us in a public place. Aldrich's "Thoughts on Flood Prevention" provides a good example for bridging the gap between Performance Studies and traditional scripted theatrical productions. As a playwright (of more traditionally structured pieces) and an adaptor, Greg Aldrich offers a solo performance piece that leans more toward the structure or arc of a play; and while it is **presentational** (a form and style that openly acknowledges itself as theatre and in which characters often speak directly to the audience), it is less self-conscious in its deployment of "research as performance" than many Performance Studies pieces are.

## Plays for Further Study

Since the 1960s, a vast number of performers—some from the world of theatre—have turned to the monologue as their primary performance mode. Perhaps the two most famous, with the longest careers, are Eric Bogosian and Spalding Gray. Female performance artists of similar import include Laurie Anderson, Karen Finley, and Holly Hughes.

Over the course of two decades (roughly 1980–2000), Eric Bogosian wrote and performed a half dozen solo pieces Off-Broadway, two of them at the New York Shakespeare Festival. He won three Obie Awards for his work, and a Drama Desk Award. His prolific career has continued into the twenty-first century, with his solo performances appearing in print, in collections of his work, and elsewhere. Bogosian is also an actor on stage, screen, and television (most notably on *Law & Order: Criminal Intent* as Captain Danny Ross), and a novelist as well. Surely his work in these other areas influences his monologues.

Spalding Gray's monologues, not without humor, explore the depths of his character, his anxieties, and his experiences. Performed at a simple table with only a glass of water on it, Gray's words speak volumes. Sadly, Gray committed suicide in 2005, and his last monologue was published posthumously, although he performed it before his death.

## CAUTION

Professionals and amateurs are hereby notified that all plays are under copyright and permission must be obtained to use them in any manner. All rights, including professional and amateur stage rights, motion picture, recitation, lecturing, public reading, radio broadcasting, television, video or sound recording, all other forms of mechanical or electronic reproduction, and the rights of translation into foreign languages, are strictly reserved. All inquiries concerning rights, including amateur rights, should be addressed to the writer or writer's agent.

# THOUGHTS ON FLOOD PREVENTION

CAST OF CHARACTERS
GREG—The playwright

SETTING—The theatre, now.

**AT RISE:** Empty stage. GREG sits at a table, Spalding Gray style, and tells the story.

### GREG

When my father was in high school in upstate New York, they told him that he would never ever go to college. He was a C student. He was failing algebra. No one in his family had ever received any higher education.

Today my father is the top Hydrologist in Alaska. Probably one of the top Hydrologists in the country.

A Hydrologist is an engineer who works with rivers. They handle flood planning. Measures slopes of mountainsides, rainfall, melting snow. They calculate probabilities, percentages. How strong does the bridge, dam, et cetera have to be to withstand that high flood of water that will happen maybe only once every fifty years. Once every hundred years. Two hundred. Equation after equation of possibility, probability.

And he really likes his job. Now, that's a polite way of saying he's somewhat a work-a-holic. See the surveying required for his job crunching numbers gave him an opportunity for what he really loves: being outdoors in the open air with nothing but nature surrounding him.

This is the only thing he had in common with my mother. My father used to spend his summers in college working at Yosemite National Park. Here he met my mother, a kinda tomboyish feminist cowgirl from Wyoming.

They were very different. See my mom was a very unconventional woman for her day. For example, she was the driving force behind one of the first Title IX lawsuits. She's a pretty amazing woman.

GREG (con't)

My father was much more conventional in expectation. He had a real John Wayne approach to masculinity. Good guys wear white hats, bad guys wear black ones. Men don't cry. That sort of stuff.

Midway through my PhD program, thinking on identity and identity construction, I find myself reflecting a lot on my father and his history. The differences and similarities between us.

He did eventually go to college and got a masters degree. But not in Hydrology as everyone supposes now. In Forestry. He's the kind of guy thinking doesn't come easy, but he works really hard and manages to figure the problem he's working on out.

I recently read about a certain test given to high school students across the world, called the Trends in International Math and Science Study. Or TIMSS for short. The TIMSS agreement—offers an extremely lengthy questionnaire at the beginning of the test. What occupation are your parents? What are your friends like? 120 questions in total. So long, students give up and stop answering questions as they go through page after page of the tedious thing.

Well, the test givers found out that the amount of questions students answered on the questionnaire directly corresponded with the math scores for the test. Statistically verifiable: people who don't give-up and finish the questionnaire get a better grade on the math portion of the test.

This is how my dad is. He doesn't get it immediately, but he struggles through until he has an answer. They thought he wouldn't graduate high school and now he is one of the top people working in a field he didn't even study in college. Helping a multitude of communities prepare for floods across the country.

Now this is a great picture I've painted, but unfortunately it's not how I see my father.

A PhD student in playwriting, my journey has been drastically different. Though I have found an interesting correlation of playwrights who have engineers as parents. See engineers are interested in how things fit together. I too am fascinated by how the parts of the world fit together, if only in stories.

(Picks up glass of water.)

GREG (con't)

The playwright Julie Jensen says that people become artists because they take things more personally than other people. They have to communicate those private, interior sorrows to find relief.

I like that. Both as a writer and as a lover of stories. I find these narratives heal me. When nothing else will. I see myself, scattered, torn apart, in the figures of others. I grieve for their failings, their shortcomings. And I feel better.

My father worked hard, because that's how he saw a man. A man was someone who provided for his family. His worth as a man came from how good a provider he was. A strong notion from his era.

My mom shared a story with me recently. My mom had been bugging my father about asking for a raise. He'd been at his first job out of college for several years now and they were still paying him the same as the day that he was hired. My dad kept telling her that that wasn't how things worked and she, not being a part of the workforce, didn't understand.

Well. My mom applied to teach Physical Education at the local University along with coaching the women's basketball team (made possible several years earlier by an aforementioned Title IX case) and asked for as much money as they would give her. As much as the male teachers and coaches.

She brought her first paycheck home to my father. It was considerably more than his. The very next day my father went into his boss's office and asked for a raise. Which, of course, they gave him, because my father is the kind of employee you don't want to lose. As my mom described it, he was all grins.

See, the man's job is to provide and he wanted, needed, to do this better than anyone. And money was a clear concept of "what you can provide" that he easily understood. The man was in charge. He was in charge of money. He was in charge of his emotions. He sat at the head of the table. He sat in his chair in the living room. His family around him.

It's strange what we remember as children. Our little minds are learning about the world. A child's mind is grasping so much, building fresh neuro-pathways.

I read last year that in the 90s they were able to cure the sight of a man who had been blind from birth. By all standards, a miracle of science. However,

GREG (con't)

his brain couldn't comprehend what he was seeing. Shapes. Color. He couldn't learn how to read them. He never learned to see.

A child's brain is a wonderful thing. It is able to do so much. Put so many ideas into patterns into a way of seeing the world.

For example, when I was little my mother used to take me and my brother to watch the women's college basketball games. My mom, the winningest coach the team has ever had to this day, was always mobbed by people who wanted to talk to her. She often shares a story of a time when she was talking with the new coach as the women warmed up, and I kept pulling on her leg. Mom, mom, mom, mom. She tries to ignore me, but I am persistent. Finally she snaps, "What is it honey?" And I stammer, "Do they ever let boys play basketball?" She laughed. But I had never seen it and I had no concept what a ridiculous question that was.

My father was gone a lot of the time growing up. Surveying for future floods. There was always a new project as the pipeline expanded, new communities were built across Alaska. New predictions had to be calculated. New probabilities considered.

So what did my child brain put together of my father? I didn't know his past or what he had come through. Just as I didn't know what my mom had come through.

What is vivid to me, to this day, is one very particular moment.

I recall crying in the stairwell at his office building. I used to hiccup when I would cry because I couldn't breathe, gasping. I don't remember over what. Most assuredly something cosmically inconsequential, like any 5-year-old might.

It was late at night. He had been working late. He always did. We were in a glass stairwell, between steps. I recall him grabbing me by the shoulders and shaking me. Men don't cry, he spat in my face. They do not cry. But I could not get a hold of myself. I could not stop hiccuping. So he just gave me a stern, disappointed glare. And released me in disgust.

This moment defined my identity. It took me a while, many years, but I did it. I stopped crying. Pure will.

GREG (con't)

In fact, I didn't cry again until college when in acting class they train you to open up to your emotions for fictitious worlds of make-believe. But I rarely cry to this day.

When I was eleven, my mother finally left my father. I had seen it coming: I had watched enough TV shows to know what shouting at each other every night and sleeping on the couch meant. My mother was never going to be the demure housewife my father had envisioned. After a decade and a half of marriage.

My father was away on another excursion to some river or other in rural Alaska. My mother resolved to be gone by the time he was back. She had a place rented, money set aside. She did not need a man to take care of her.

When he came home to an empty house: his wife and children gone, he was devastated. All he had worked to build had been ripped away from him. He was no longer the provider.

Every night my father sat in his chair and wept continuously, tears streaming over his eye lids washing his cheeks raw and red. I found it uncomfortable to look at him. I was embarrassed for him. He would want hugs, physical contact. He would extend his arms to me, the tears dampening his shirt. But all I could think was, Men don't cry. They. Do not. Cry.

What do you do when everything you have built is torn away in a sudden incalculable flow of water? Your math was wrong. The flood that was only supposed to happen every one hundred, two hundred years? It's here.

I still hate being vulnerable. That's an odd thing for a writer to say. You have to be to tell stories. You are every time. It's why I love it. And why I fear it. Why I have dedicated my life to it.

I am more nervous to share this story to you tonight than I hope I am letting on.

I suppose I am more concerned with what happens after the flood than before. Because there are things that we aren't prepared for. And I do not always know how to get through them.

And I don't know what you are struggling with tonight, but I hope in some small way sharing this story helps.

**END OF PLAY**

# Solo Playwriting: An Exercise on Solo Performance

1. Recall how Aldrich described the experience when as a small child he cried and hiccupped, and what a lasting impression that moment had on him.
2. Think of equally compelling moments in your life. List them.
3. Write one to two paragraphs describing in detail your favorite from the list.
4. Read your piece aloud to yourself or others.

# For Further Research

Bial, Henry, and Sara Brady. *The Performance Studies Reader*. 3rd ed. New York: Routledge, 2015.

Bruno, Sean, and Luke Dixon *Creating Solo Performance*. New York: Routledge, 2015.

Bogosian, Eric. *100 (Monologues)*. New York: Theatre Communications Group, 2014.

———. *Pounding Nails in the Floor with My Forehead*. New York: Theatre Communications Group, 2008.

———. *The Essential Bogosian: Talk Radio, Drinking in America, FunHouse and Men Inside*. New York: Theatre Communications Group, 1994.

Catron, Louis E. *The Power of One: The Solo Play for Playwrights, Actors, and Directors*. Reissue ed. Long Grove, IL: Waveland Press, 2009.

Gray, Spalding. *Life Interrupted: The Unfinished Monologue*. New York: Crown Publishers, 2005.

———. *Swimming to Cambodia*. New York: Theatre Communications Group, 2005.

———. *Gray's Anatomy*. New York: Vintage Books, 1993.

———. *Monster in a Box*. New York: Vintage Books, 1992.

Schechner, Richard. *Performance Studies: An Introduction*. 3rd ed. New York: Routledge, 2013.

# CHAPTER 6

# Marnie J. Glazier

## PLAYWRIGHT

## *BOIS DENTELLE*

©2015 Marnie J. Glazier

## CAST OF CHARACTERS
### THE ENSEMBLE

## PLAYWRIGHT'S NOTE

This play is meant to be performed before an exhibition of various "tree" works—paintings, sculptures, prints, digital installation, etc.—to be determined by the nature of the performance space. The play can be performed by one or many ENSEMBLE MEMBERS, and it has the capacity to engage the creator(s) of the visual works in performance. The following script is written for solo performance with accompanying digital installation.

# *EUCALYPTUS*

©2015 Marnie J. Glazier

CAST OF CHARACTERS
THE ENSEMBLE

## PLAYWRIGHT'S NOTE

This piece is research-driven and ideally should be accompanied by a visual exhibit/installation/illustration.

# *EASTERN COTTONWOOD*

©2015 Marnie J. Glazier

CAST OF CHARACTERS
THE ENSEMBLE

SETTING—Lecture Hall

## PRODUCTION HISTORY

"Bois Dentelle," "Eucalyptus," and "Eastern Cottonwood" were all written as part of the 31 Plays in 31 Days challenge organized by Rachel Bublitz and were first performed at the first-ever Fuller Future Festival in honor of Buckminster Fuller at Southern Illinois University in July 2012.

# About the Playwright

Originally from Connecticut, Marnie J. Glazier has lived in many places. She received her BA in American Studies and her MA in English from Trinity College in Hartford, Connecticut; her MFA from the University of Iowa; and her PhD from Southern Illinois University Carbondale, where she focused on both performance studies and theatre theory and practice. She has taught in Denver and the Twin Cities. She presently resides in California, where she teaches theatre and directs at Hartnell College. As a teaching artist and writer, Marnie explores interdisciplinary, boundary-crossing creative inquiry and devised theatre. She has served as a guest artist at the Minneapolis-based In the Heart of the Beast Puppet and Mask Theatre, and more recently with The Western Stage in Salinas, California. She has also collaborated with El Teatro Campesino. As an environmental activist and eco-theatre practitioner, Marnie is an ongoing member of the Performance and Ecology group at the American Society for Theatre Research, where her dance performance/installation *Transpiration* appeared. Her dissertation, entitled *Eco-theatre and New Media: Devising Toward Transnational Balance,* married her dedication to eco-theatre, new media, and devising. She also presents regularly at the Eugene O'Neill Society's international conference, where she has discussed the environment as expressed in O'Neill's plays.

# Form and Style

"Bois Dentelle," "Eucalyptus," and "Eastern Cottonwood" are part of a curated series of "Tree Plays" that Glazier wrote to express both her deep concern for the care-taking of our planet and her passion for educating audiences about environmental issues. Play scripts and performances of this ilk are often classified as **ecodrama**. Each tree in the cycle presents a different issue, environmental or otherwise. "Bois Dentelle" offers us an endangered species and reminds us of biodiversity, while "Eucalyptus" illustrates that both the life-affirming and the toxic sometimes paradoxically coexist, and in "Eastern Cottonwood" the tree's pollination procedure is aptly and humorously compared to human reproduction. Some of Glazier's other plays have more deliberately emanated from collective writing situations. In these settings, as with a piece called *Beauty* that she shaped with a cast of young women in response to Eve Ensler's *The Vagina Monologues,* she works with an ensemble to create a piece and then shapes their work, carefully crafting a production. While the short pieces included here might read as monologues, the playwright notes that they are just as well suited to ensemble performance, and she comments on how employing an installation/exhibit enhances their production. The first two plays have a dance-like quality, and we can envision the use of media along with the interdisciplinarity inherent in all three. Also inherent in these short plays is their documentary quality. As a genre, docudramas frequently utilize data, facts, sometimes charts and graphs, and, today, digital media to put their messages across.

# Plays for Further Study

Any play that foregrounds environmental concerns would couple nicely with the pieces by Glazier included here. Glazier, and Downing Cless before her, have examined canonical pieces from this standpoint, and both have directed, for example, Aristophanes's *The Birds* to this end. It is difficult to locate devised texts in print, as they tend to be venue-based and issue-based, performance-dependent, and often unpublished. Stylistically, Ntozake Shange's *spell #7* offers a good example. To historically contextualize Glazier's use of data, a look at Living Newspapers from the Federal Theatre Project would be appropriate. Moises Kaufman's *The Laramie Project* and Anna Deveare Smith's *Twilight: Los Angeles, 1992* and *Fires in the Mirror* are all interview-based theatre, which has recently come to be termed verbatim theatre.

## CAUTION

Professionals and amateurs are hereby notified that all plays are under copyright and permission must be obtained to use them in any manner. All rights, including professional and amateur stage rights, motion picture, recitation, lecturing, public reading, radio broadcasting, television, video or sound recording, all other forms of mechanical or electronic reproduction, and the rights of translation into foreign languages, are strictly reserved. All inquiries concerning rights, including amateur rights, should be addressed to the writer or writer's agent.

# BOIS DENTELLE

CAST OF CHARACTERS
THE ENSEMBLE

ENSEMBLE

Bois Dentelle.

(Beat.)

A lesson in silvics …

(Digital installation begins.)

According to the American Forests Organization, "Biodiversity is the key to health." The Biodiversity Conservation Network defines biodiversity as "the variety of all forms of life on earth … A necessity, not a luxury."

(Reads the following lengthy quote.)

"Biodiversity not only provides direct benefits like food, medicine, and energy; it also affords us a 'life support system.' Biodiversity is required for the recycling of essential elements, such as carbon, oxygen, and nitrogen. It is also responsible for mitigating pollution, protecting watersheds, and combating soil erosion. Because biodiversity acts as a buffer against excessive variations in weather and climate, it protects us from catastrophic events beyond human control. … The importance of biodiversity to a healthy environment has become increasingly clear. We have learned that the future well being of all humanity depends on our stewardship of the Earth. … When we overexploit living resources, we threaten our own survival." …

(Digital installation climaxes.)

ENSEMBLE (con't)

Most of us learned when we were children in school, that trees produce oxygen. And yet that most basic lesson, for all of its import—for all of its fascinatingly simple miraculousness ... is among the most easily forgotten ...

(Beat. Shift in installation.)

There are thousands of known species of tree in the world, and over a thousand among them are critically endangered. ... We talk about endangered species, but like London-based botanist, Sara Oldfield says, "Often animals are discussed, but what about the plants on which they depend?" ...

(Beat. Shift in installation. Bois Dentelle.)

Have you seen the Bois Dentelle? There are only two of these beautiful trees left in the world. ...

> The following quote is projected at the close of the digital installation, along with web addresses, and the statement, "To find out more about what you can do to save the trees, visit the following websites. "... americanforests.org; worldwildlife. org; forestry.gov.uk; unep.org; arborday.org; bgci.org. "Biodiversity and the issues that affect it cross all national borders." ...

**END OF PLAY**

# EUCALYPTUS

CAST OF CHARACTERS
   THE ENSEMBLE

ENSEMBLE

The irony of the eucalyptus is in its long symbology. It represents, of all things, prudence,

   (Beat.)

as well as protection, healing, nurturing.

   (Unfolds a source page.)

From Magical Revelations.webs.com:

   (Reads.)

"The name [eucalyptus] is derived from the Greek word, 'eucalyptos' which means 'well-covered.' This name refers to the protective membrane that covers the budding flowers of the tree."

   (New page. New source.)

The Native Americans' Web-ring honors eucalyptus as a "life-giving tree."

   (Flipping to a new page. New source.)

At the same time, Randy Ananda's *Alien Forest, Alien Ocean, Alien Sky,* points to bioengineering agri-giant Monsanto and its subsidiaries' USDA approval of "260,000 genetically engineered eucalyptus trees" across the southeast US—in Texas, Mississippi, Louisiana, Florida, Georgia, and South Carolina—asking us

ENSEMBLE (con't)

to "Imagine our declining pollinators—bees, moths, butterflies, and bats—coming upon thousands of acres of toxic trees, genetically engineered so that every cell in the tree exudes pesticide, from crown to root. Imagine a world without pollinators. Without seed disbursers. Without soil microbes.

It would be a silent forest, a killing forest, an alien forest." ...

(Putting down the source materials.)

The irony of the eucalyptus is in its physiognomy. A fast-growing tree that can reach exorbitant heights in comparatively little time, eucalyptus are easily cultivated but also have the potential to be "invasive water-suckers."

(Lifting and flipping to a new page. New source.)

News source Voice of America talks about the eucalyptus introduced to South Africa in the nineteenth century.

(Reading.)

"to grow for props in gold mines" and their disastrous effects on the South African ecosystem. "[Eucalyptus] are mostly evergreen, so they suck water from the ground ... from 80–200 liters a day. ... In addition to using more water ... [they're] often allelopathic. ... They kill off surrounding plant-life by releasing a chemical into the soil, to which local plants have no resistance." ...

(Putting down the source materials.)

Yet another irony ... Monsanto and Arborgen's GM forests have received the neat genetic modification of toxicity, containing the bt toxin—

ENSEMBLE (con't)
(Lifting and flipping to a new page. New source.)

What CBS News' Smriti Rao calls

(Reading.)

"a genetic tweak that prevents the trees from reproducing."

(Beat. Reading.)

"In the case of the eucalyptus trees, Arborgen restricts their pollen production with a bacterial gene that produces a toxic enzyme called barnase that slices apart genetic material in a cell, causing death." ...

(Putting down the source materials.)

The "life-tree," the tree of prudence, protection, healing, nurturing ... has a new potential ... to become the tree of death. In the words of Randy Ananda,

(Reading.)

"GM contamination occurs around the globe. The technology cannot be contained. Genetically modified organisms are dominant over natural species and will forever alter earth's natural plants." ...

(Putting down the source materials. Looking at audience. Beat.)

If ... we let them. ...

(Silence.)

**END OF PLAY**

# EASTERN COTTONWOOD

CAST OF CHARACTERS
　THE ENSEMBLE

　SETTING—Lecture Hall

**AT RISE:** The ENSEMBLE MEMBER is dressed conservatively, something of the schoolmarm or librarian, hair up, glasses, shirt tucked in and buttoned up to the top, cardigan sweater, etc. SHE holds a pointer and stands before an easel displaying the diagrams which illustrate HER lessons.

ENSEMBLE MEMBER

Now ... for a lesson in sex education.

　(Clears HER throat. Flips to a page on her easel. Illustration.)

Today we will discuss the cottonwood tree.

　(Turns and indicates with HER pointer.)

The cottonwood is a *dioecious* tree.

　(Flips the page. Clears HER throat.)

As is the case with human ... sexual reproduction ... there are male and female cottonwood trees. Generally speaking ...

ENSEMBLE MEMBER (con't)
(Flips the page again)
Like human females, female cottonwood trees produce ... seeds.

(Flips page.)

Like human males, male cottonwood trees ... produce pollen.

(Loosens HER collar. Beat.)

Sexual reproduction among cottonwoods is among the most passionate of endeavors.

(Unbuttons and slips off HER sweater. Flips the page. Losing HERSELF in the moment. Huskily.)

If I could be any tree, I'd be the eastern cottonwood.

(Remembering HERSELF. Flips the page to reveal text, quote from Treeservice.com. Reading, rapturously.)

The cottonwood tree seed is the seed that stays in flight the longest ...

(Loosens the clip in HER hair. Shakes HER head and flips the page to reveal the remainder of the quote. Reads, savoring each word.)

The tiny seed is surrounded by ultra-light, white fluff hairs

(Taking off HER glasses as SHE finishes this last.)

that can carry it on the air for several days ...

ENSEMBLE MEMBER (con't)
(Pauses, breathing heavily. Collects HERSELF, and flips the page to reveal the final illustration and quote.)

Small wonder ... trees are the oldest living organisms on earth ...

## END OF PLAY

# Group Collaboration: An Exercise on Collective Creation

The Living Newspaper

Some Elements in Living Newspapers

- Use of projections
- Sound (cues, instrumental music, song)
- Poetry and prose (fiction)
- Voice-overs
- Data
- Prototypical characters (epithets and not names)

1. As a group, select a current issue. Find an online article about a "hot topic" that might serve as the basis for your group performance.
2. Select images, music, as well as lines from the article that all make a similar point.
3. Create a collage of the material you have gathered, and then put it in some sort of logical order for presenting, combining live actors with the bulleted elements above.
4. Present your Living Newspaper to others.

For other exercises on devising, see "Exploration Two: Playwriting and Types of Plays" in Fletcher, Anne, and Scott R. Irelan. *Experiencing Theatre*. Cambridge, MA: Hackett Publishing, 2015.

# For Further Research

Arons, Wendy, and Theresa J. May, eds. *Readings in Performance and Ecology*. New York: Palgrave McMillan, 2012.

Bicât, Tina, and Chris Baldwin eds. *Devised and Collaborative Theatre: A Practical Guide*. Ramsbury, UK: Crowood Press, 2002.

Cless, Downing. *Ecology and Environment in European Drama.* Routledge, London UK., 2011.

Kershaw, Baz. *Theatre Ecology: Environments and Performance Events.* Cambridge, UK: Cambridge University Press, 2009.

# CHAPTER 7

# Jacob Juntunen

PLAYWRIGHT

## *BLACK AND WHITE*
©2015 Jacob Juntunen

**PRODUCTION HISTORY**

*Black and White* premiered in 2015 as part of Southern Illinois University's Big Muddy Shorts, a monthly festival for the performance of original short plays.

CAST OF CHARACTERS
    USHER
    MAN 1
    WOMAN 1
    WOMAN 2
    WOMAN 3
    WOMAN 4
    MAN 2
    MANAGER

SETTING—The Crystal Palace Theatre

# About the Playwright

Originally from California, with a BA from Reed College and advanced degrees from Ohio University (MA) and Northwestern University (PhD), Jacob Juntunen heads the Playwriting programs at Southern Illinois University. He has extensive experience in the Chicago storefront theatre scene as an alumnus Senior Network Playwright at Chicago Dramatists, as the founding managing director of Mortar Theatre, and as a recipient of a Community Arts Assistance Program (CAAP) grant. His play *Hath Taken Away* (O'Neill Conference semifinalist; Source Festival finalist) was read at the Last Frontier Theatre Conference, at Chicago Dramatists, and at Will Geer's Theatricum Botanicum. *In the Shadow of His Language* (Kendeda Graduate Playwriting Competition finalist; O'Neill Conference semifinalist; Princess Grace semifinalist) was read at Chicago Dramatists, the Alliance Theatre, and Playwrights Horizons. Other plays include *Joan's Laughter, Under America,* and *Saddam's Lions* (this last play is included in Eric Lane and Nina Shengold's compilation entitled *Plays for Two*). Juntunen's play *See Him?* was included in the Belarusian Dream Theater (a project in which eighteen theatres in thirteen countries simultaneously produced plays to raise awareness about human rights violations in Belarus). His academic essays and reviews have appeared in *Theatre Journal, Puppetry International, Polish-AngloSaxon Studies, Peace & Change,* and the *LMDA Review.* His scholarship is also included in several anthologies. He was awarded a 2011 Faculty Fulbright Fellowship to Adam Mickiewicz University in Poznań, Poland; a 2014 Thesaurus Poloniae Senior Scholar Fellowship to spend three months researching in Kraków, and a Collaborative SEED Grant from SIU to analyze the archives of Polish theatre auteur Tadeusz Kantor. Juntunen's book *Mainstream AIDS Theatre, the Media, and Gay Civil Rights: Making the Radical Palatable* was published in 2016 by Routledge.

# Form and Style

The play's title both references and troubles a frequently and carelessly uttered phrase about issues being "black and white." Juntunen addresses numerous critical social issues, especially regarding racial identity and self-identification, in a scant five pages. He historicizes contemporary racial protest and problems by setting the play in a time when segregation was commonplace and miscegenation laws prohibited interracial marriage—in this way distancing us a bit from the play's action, yet at the same time leaving space for us to recognize the subtle (and not so subtle) ways in which discrimination is prevalent today. Characters in "Black and White" embody their racial identities: one, when asked what color he is, responds, "Caramel?" and another, when confronted with the audience segregation that serves as the play's underpinning, declares, "Maybe I'll just stand in the middle." Interestingly, physical space in the play mirrors the racial divide, with the segregation that existed in the United States represented in the play by the usher's thwarted attempt to categorize characters by color and to sort them into two locations. In addition to confronting racism, "Black and White" alludes to anti-Semitism, serving to remind us that people are often stereotyped and marginalized by race, class, ethnicity, gender, and religion. Ironically, the concert the characters attend is cancelled because upon his arrival, the famed clarinetist and bandleader Benny Goodman (offstage and not in the play's action) was revealed to be Jewish and thus prohibited from performing at this venue.

Socioeconomic concerns and class are illustrated in the play by talk of finances and the usher's fear of being fired. He excuses his complicity in racism by attempting to empathize with the other characters and by stating that he needs this job to pay his mortgage. In his appearance at the play's conclusion, the manager utters a veiled threat: "How's your new house?". Rather than giving the characters proper names, the playwright has chosen to assign them epithets (Woman 1, Man 1, etc.), a **theatrical convention** (a rule about the world of the play) that cuts across centuries of theatre history, a technique whereby a single character type can stand for many of its category. The usher's repeated refrain—"Welcome to the Crystal Palace! General admission is standing room only, so whites over here, and blacks over there"—recalls the call-and-response of slave songs and perhaps church services, a technique we can also observe in protest dramas of the Great Depression, the 1960s, or 2017.

# Plays for Further Study

Racial identity—in fact, identity and classification—has been a part of American drama almost since its infancy. Dion Boucicault's *The Octoroon*, a Civil War era melodrama, focuses on miscegenation as a plantation owner's son has fallen in love with a young woman who is one-eighth black, an octoroon (Note Juntunen's allusion to the drop of blood that determines race in "Black and White."). The play's heroine, Zoe, has been educated and raised by the plantation owners, but the homestead is now heavily mortgaged to the villain. Before the truth comes out that money to save the plantation is on its way, Zoe kills herself rather than face the humiliation of the slave auction block. *The Octoroon* includes other racial identifications, as it incorporates significant Irish and Native American roles. Alice Childress's realistic drama *Wedding Band: A Love/Hate Story in Black and White* (1962) centers on miscegenation as well. Set in South Carolina in 1918, the story depicts a long-term interracial relationship that must be kept secret. College actors find the drama compelling and the characters rich even today. As Juntunen did with the title of his play, Leslie Lee complicates a demeaning phrase that refers to blacks' alleged propensity for tardiness with his 1962 *Colored People's Time*. Reminiscent of the vaudeville stage, the script comprises thirteen vignettes tracing the black experience in the United States; in this history-based piece, each sketch zeroes in on a particular moment, such as the Montgomery, Alabama bus boycott. Poet Langston Hughes's short verse play *Scottsboro Limited* (1931) was the playwright's response to the unfair charge waged against eight black youths accused of raping two young white women on a train. It resonates today with current issues regarding prejudice against black youth on the part of the US judicial system. This play reverberates with call-and-response dialogue utilized in the name of protest within, agit-prop (agitation and propaganda) theatre. Hughes's *The Mulatto* (1935) partners well with "Black and White" for different reasons: Playwright Hughes interrogates miscegenation and the ways in which children of mixed-race negotiate their racial identities.

Many, many plays deal with race relations and identity construction, and "Black and White" could be paired with any number of them. Juntunen's play encapsulates issues that have plagued us as a people for generations, and the work would be a welcome addition to the study of Black Theatre. Some other plays and playwrights to consider are plays by Lynn Nottage, especially *Intimate Apparel*; any play by Suzan-Lori Parks; the political and protest plays of Amiri Baraka (birth name Leroi Jones); the plays of August Wilson; and, of course, the timeless *A Raisin in the Sun* by Lorraine Hansberry.

## CAUTION

# BLACK AND WHITE

CAST OF CHARACTERS
    USHER
    MAN 1
    WOMAN 1
    WOMAN 2
    WOMAN 3
    WOMAN 4
    MAN 2
    MANAGER

    SETTING—The Crystal Palace Theatre

**AT RISE:** USHER is alone onstage when MAN 1 and WOMAN 1 enter.

USHER
Welcome to the Crystal Palace! General admission is standing room only, so whites over here, and blacks over there. The concert will start momentarily.

(MAN 1 and WOMAN 1 both move stage right.)

Oh, I'm sorry, ma'am. The white section is over there.

WOMAN 1
I know.

MAN 1
What's the problem?

USHER

Look, I'm sorry, I don't make the rules. I don't care where people stand, but if my manager sees people mixing, I'll get fired.

MAN 1

We're here on a date, we don't want to make any problems.

USHER

Listen, I understand. I got married a couple months ago, a baby's already on the way, and we used all our savings to put a down-payment on a house. The laws that say you two can't be married in this state are horrible, I always vote for the candidate that says he'll change them, and, again, if it were up to me you could stand where ever you—

WOMAN 1

I'm black.

USHER

Okay, yeah, I feel solidarity, too, but—

MAN 1

You white people made the laws. One drop of blood.

USHER

But she's paler than I am—

(WOMAN 2 enters.)

WOMAN 1

Over here!

(WOMAN 1 and 2 hug.)

WOMAN 1 (con't)
This idiot wants me to stand in the whites only section.

WOMAN 2
What a lump.

USHER
I can't get fired, I've got a new mortgage to pay and an usher doesn't get paid much—

WOMAN 2
She's my sister.

USHER
You're joking.

WOMAN 1
White people get mad when I try to pass, and get mad when I try to be black.

USHER
Is this Candid Camera?

MAN 1
Get bent.

(WOMAN 3 enters.)

USHER
Welcome to the Crystal Palace! General admission is standing room only, so whites over here, and blacks over there. The concert will start momentarily.

WOMAN 3
I'm not.

USHER

Not what?

WOMAN 3

White or black.

USHER

You have to be one or the other.

MAN 1

Stand with us.

WOMAN 3

Maybe I'll just stand in the middle.

USHER

You can't stand in the aisle. If the manager comes—

MAN 1 and WOMAN 1

You'll get fired.

WOMAN 2

Give us a break.

(WOMAN 4 enters.)

USHER

Welcome to the Crystal Palace! General admission is standing room only, so whites over here, and blacks over there. The concert will start momentarily.

WOMAN 4

I'm down! Brown is my color! Latina is my identifier!

WOMAN 3

Stand in the aisle with me.

USHER

No, no, no!

WOMAN 4

When do the cats start blowing?

MAN 1

It should have already started.

USHER

My manager will be up here soon to check on everything, and I can't have you in the black section—

WOMAN 1

But I'm black!

USHER

And no one can be in the aisle!

(Enter MAN 2.)

Welcome to the Crystal Palace! General admission is standing room only, so whites over here, and blacks over ... So go ... Go over ... I'm sorry, sir, what color are you?

MAN 2

Caramel?

USHER

Okay! Look! I don't care what's in your blood! I don't care who your ancestors are! I don't care about anything except how dark your skin is! I need all of you with dark skin over here, and all of you with light skin over here so I don't get fired!

WOMAN 4

What do you mean by light?

WOMAN 3

Yeah, I'm sort of light-ish.

USHER

No! Just—! I CAN'T LOSE MY JOB!

(MANAGER enters.)

MANAGER

What's going on up here?

USHER

Please, sir, don't fire me! I've been trying to get them to—

MANAGER

Everyone, listen up. I'm afraid the concert's been canceled. We don't allow Jews in here, and somehow no one figured out Benny Goodman was Jewish until he got here.

MAN 1

Are we getting refunds?

MANAGER

Your tickets are fully refundable.

(All exit except USHER and MANAGER.)

USHER

Sorry, sir, I just—

MANAGER

Shut up. Go downstairs and help with crowd control.

USHER

Yes, sir.

MANAGER

Make sure the blacks and whites get in the right lines.

USHER

I'm not sure it's quite as simple as—

MANAGER

How's your new house?

USHER

Very nice.

MANAGER

So?

USHER

I'll go downstairs and help with crowd control.

(Blackout.)

## END OF PLAY

# What Do You See?: An Exercise on Image Tracking

Image tracking can help readers in analyzing any play, and it can be practiced easily with a short piece like "Black and White."

1. Identify each and every instance of words that express the following:
   Blood, ancestry
   Color
   Physical place or position (line, aisle, etc.)
   Money
2. Count the number of references to each you found.
3. Think about how the playwright consciously included this many in so few pages.
4. See if you can use these repeated images to write about one of the play's thematic concerns. This can take the form of a monologue or a two character play.
5. Share.

# For Further Research

Dickerson, Glenda. *African American Theatre: A Cultural Companion*. Cambridge, UK, and Malden, MA: Polity, 2008.

Elam, Harry J., and David Krasner eds. *African American Performance and Theater History: A Critical Reader*. Oxford, UK: Oxford University Press, 2001.

Hay, Samuel A. *African American Theatre: An Historical and Critical Analysis*. Cambridge, UK: Cambridge University Press, 1994.

Hill, Errol G., and James V. Hatch. *A History of African American Theater*. Cambridge, UK: Cambridge University Press, 2006.

Young, Harvey, ed. *The Cambridge Companion to African American Theater*. Cambridge, UK: Cambridge University Press, Cambridge, 2013.

# CHAPTER 8

# David Dudley

### PLAYWRIGHT

## *UPROOTING OAKS*

©2016 David Dudley

**PRODUCTION HISTORY**

"Uprooting Oaks" was first seen on April 7, 2016, as a staged reading for Southern Illinois University's Big Muddy Shorts, a monthly festival for the performance of original short plays.

CAST OF CHARACTERS
  TIM
  TIM'S SOUL
  SLUG

  SETTING—A bare stage

# About the Playwright

David Dudley is a playwright, journalist, and educator. His short plays have been performed in New York, Boston, California, Chicago, Arizona, and Vermont. *Gorillas in the Sky*, a full-length play, was a finalist at the WordBRIDGE Playwrights Lab and a semifinalist at the Seven Devils Playwrights Conference. His play *Funeral for a Salamander* was also named semifinalist at the Seven Devils Playwrights Conference. As a journalist, he has had articles published in *American Theatre Magazine, The Christian Science Monitor, Contemporary Theatre Review (UK), Conjunto Theatre Journal (Cuba),* and the *Vermont Chronicle*. David received a BFA in Playwriting from DePaul University. He served as a script reader for Steppenwolf Theater and trained as an apprentice with both Bread and Puppet Theater and with The Wooster Group. David currently resides in Carbondale, Illinois, where he is pursuing his MFA in playwriting at Southern Illinois University. He lives with his son, Ricky.

# Form and Style

In "Uprooting Oaks," we find Tim sleeping as his soul searches for the answers to life's most important questions: How can I be the best husband to my wife? How do I best raise my child? How does someone avoid a bullet heading directly toward his head? Although Tim's body cannot move, his senses are acutely aware that gunfire is coming from his neighbor's apartment, and that a bullet destined for his head is coming from that direction. This revelation sends Tim's soul reeling through his memories: the good and the bad, all of it unpredictable and uncontrollable. As Tim's soul struggles to make meaning of a life on the verge of ending too soon, his final analysis yields the question we all will certainly face in our final moments. What answer will Tim's soul find?

So, where does a playwright come up with such an intense topic for a play? In this case, the idea came from David Dudley's daily, lived experience. In the early morning on Easter Sunday 2016, a stray bullet killed forty-one-year-old Timothy Scott Beaty. At first, the media reported that Beaty was in bed when the bullet hit him. As both the police and the media did more investigating, however, it became clear that

Beaty had, in fact, given two students shelter in his home after they fled the house party next door, once shots were fired during an altercation outside the neighboring residence. Apparently, he was killed while protecting them. His wife and son survive him. Dudley wrote this particular play as a way to wrestle with his own feelings over such a senseless act of violence. Like many other playwrights working in the area of Theatrical Realism, Dudley uses his own life as an inspiration point for his writing. What makes Dudley different from those working in Realism, however, is the way that Dudley chooses to abstract the actual occurrence and subsequent media accounts of the events through techniques of both Italian Futurism and Magical Realism. He does this not to take away from the horror of the actual incident, but rather as a way to invite us into a larger dialogue about the issue at hand.

In using elements of both Realism and non-Realism, Dudley has given us a wonderful example of the hybrid play that is much more non-Realism than Realism in its form and style. Italian Futurism was a movement that emerged sometime around 1909 when Filippo Tommaso Marinetti penned his Futurist Manifesto. The Futurists were interested in breaking free of the conventions of the day by offering **sintesi** (brief, compressed plays) as part of **serata** (an evening's entertainment). The form and style of **Futurism** in live theatre often abandoned logic and reason, commingling imagination and daily life. Time and space are not necessarily chronological, and characters are often animals, sounds, or even inanimate objects. The year 1925 seems to be when the term **Magical (or Magic) Realism** was first used by Franz Roh, a German art critic. Roh was discussing a new kind of painting technique that signaled that the Expressionist style was coming to an end. What Roh was articulating was an approach to art-making that commingles elements of daily life with the fantastical, the natural world with supernatural happenings—all with people reacting as if this is not at all unusual. That is, in a world that otherwise looks and sounds similar to the one we experience, fantasy is not questioned. It is accepted. By the 1950s, novelists such as Jorge Luis Borges and Italo Calvino were utilizing elements of Magical Realism in their writing. Playwrights also looked to Magical Realism for another way to tell stories. Some attributes of plays using Magic Realism include nonhuman characters, a sense of timelessness, and moments of the "unreal" becoming "real" (for example, someone's soul talking to us).

# Plays for Further Study

*Marisol* by José Rivera is an excellent example of how Magical Realism can work in live theatre. In this case, the play takes us into the New York life of Marisol and her guardian angel. *Angels in America* by Tony Kushner is another good play text to look at in terms of how elements of Magical Realism can influence the way a story is told. As the title indicates, angels just might be the key to unlocking the form at work in Kushner's play. Playwright Sarah Ruhl's *The Clean House* gives us a script that includes snow falling indoors and apples dropping from the sky into the living room. The occurrences are normal within the otherwise realistic world that Ruhl creates. *The Magic Rainforest: An Amazon Journey* by José Cruz González features the young boy Aki and his quest to save the Amazon rain forest. Birds, plants, other animals, and the wind help him along the way. Given the nature of the Futurist impulse, a "full-length" Futurist play is only one or two pages long. "Detonation" by Francesco Cangiullo and "Feet" by Filippo Marinetti are two favorite examples of Italian Futurism. In the first, Cangiullo has as his sole character "a bullet"; and in the second, Marinetti shows the public only legs in action, regardless of dialogue. The neo-Futurists have kept the spirit of Marinetti's ideas alive in contemporary times with short plays such as "Hemingway Afternoon" and "Black-Eyed Susans."

## CAUTION

Professionals and amateurs are hereby notified that all plays are under copyright and permission must be obtained to use them in any manner. All rights, including professional and amateur stage rights, motion picture, recitation, lecturing, public reading, radio broadcasting, television, video or sound recording, all other forms of mechanical or electronic reproduction, and the rights of translation into foreign languages, are strictly reserved. All inquiries concerning rights, including amateur rights, should be addressed to the writer or writer's agent.

# UPROOTING OAKS

***For Tim Beaty and all those whose lives were stolen away by stray bullets.

CAST OF CHARACTERS
>TIM—A man, sleeping
>TIM'S SOUL—An embodiment, searching
>SLUG—Bullet from a 9mm pistol

>SETTING—A bare stage

**AT RISE:** A bare stage. A man, TIM, lays in bed, asleep. TIM'S SOUL addresses audience.

### TIM'S SOUL

Good evening, everybody. My name is Tim, and I'm asleep. Now, I know what you're thinking: If he's asleep, how is he talking to us? Funny you should ask. See, that's Tim. I'm his soul; the part of him that doesn't sleep. Ever. When Tim sleeps, I keep on working. I'm the one who wrestles with Tim's unsolvable problems: How do I keep my wife, Susie, happy, for instance. And, how do I raise my five-year-old son, Michel, to be a man—a good man, one who contributes meaningfully to society, while still being able to pursue his own bliss. Or, since Tim is a drummer, I spend a lot of time trying to figure out drum patterns. Trying to find ways to ride the waves of lyrics, or to become the ground on which the lyrics can dance. If the drum most closely resembles the human heartbeat—boom, bap—you could say that Tim's heart and his drums are one.

But tonight's different. There's a party next door. People are having a good time. It's three a.m. The festive mood with which the evening began is giving way to exhaustion, frustration, and the need to fight—or fuck. Excuse my language. I am a soul, after all. I don't censor myself for anybody. If you don't like it, go fuck yourself. Lest I digress. I can tell from the loud, angry voices, that fucking isn't for everyone. I know something bad's about to happen, but I'm helpless to do anything about it.

SLUG

Bang!

(Enter SLUG, moving slowly on a trajectory towards TIM.)

TIM'S SOUL

Did you hear that? Gunshot.

SLUG

I'm a 9mm slug. I've just been kicked out of the chamber. I don't have a soul, nor do I feel things. I do what I'm told. I was made for one thing and one thing only: to kill.

(TIM shifts in his sleep.)

TIM'S SOUL

Slug's headed directly towards me. Though I'm asleep, I can feel it whizzing and whirring through the air. We are on a crash course towards each other. How can an immobile object be on a crash course with anything, you ask? Right now, this very moment, we are all on a crash course with some great celestial mass that exists beyond the range of our current astronomic vision. Our galaxy and millions of galaxies just like it are streaming towards that mass, pulled by gravity, at more than 400 miles per second. We appear to be still, but we are moving.

SLUG

I know how that goes. Look at me right now. Do I appear to be moving? Time moves more slowly for me than for you. You're so slow, everything whips past you. I'm so fast that everything around me appears to stop.

TIM'S SOUL

Though it doesn't look like it, I know death is near.

SLUG

Yes. I'm on a crash course with your head. And this cheap drywall, these pipes, and these support beams can't stop me.

(SLUG battles through the wall separating the apartments. TIM's leg twitches.)

TIM'S SOUL

I can hear the drywall crumbling as the slug passes through it. Life flashes before my eyes: I'm in a dark place, warm and wet and perfectly peaceful. Then a shaft of light cuts through the darkness. A big, rough hand takes hold of my ankle and pulls me out. I'm cold; I scream:

TIM

(As a baby)
Wah! Wahhh!

TIM'S SOUL

The first time I was the victim of unprovoked violence, but not the last.

SLUG

It's a shame you look so peaceful in your sleep. I'm bad news.

TIM'S SOUL

Now, I'm in Ms. Guerrero's fifth-grade English class. She reads aloud from Sappho. Nobody's paying attention. But then she sees that I'm hanging on her every word. She looks me in the eye as she reads, slowly:

SLUG

(As Ms. Guerrero)
Eros harrows my heart:
wild gales sweeping desolate
mountains,
uprooting oaks.

TIM'S SOUL

My body fights to escape scratchy, tight-fitting denim.

(Beat.)

My first erection. For the right reason. That I remember.

(Beat.)

Now I'm running the bases on a muddy baseball diamond. My best friend from high-school, Mike, for whom my son was named, chases me round the bases. He and Jerry sling mud at me. I laugh …

TIM

(Laughs)

TIM'S SOUL

… until they catch me. They hit me once …

(TIM writhes with each "Splat".)

SLUG

Splat

TIM'S SOUL

They hit me again. And again and again

SLUG

Splat splat splat

TIM'S SOUL

And again and again and again and again

                           SLUG

Splat splat splat splat splat!


                        TIM'S SOUL

They won't stop. I'm helpless to make them stop. They won't fucking stop!


        (Then, calm, resigned.)


I weep.


                           SLUG

Not much time left, now.


                        TIM'S SOUL

Tucson, Arizona. Gong's ghetto. Susie and I kiss through the bedroom window
of her father's trailer-home. Gunshots ring out. I fall to the ground. An engine
screams. Tires peel. Drive-by. Five bullet-holes in the trailer. It's a miracle that
Susie and I aren't hit.


                           SLUG

Crash landing in 3 …


                        TIM'S SOUL

A week later. In that very room, in bed. Our bodies become one. She smiles,
looks me directly in the eye. Ms. Guerrero's voice comes back to me:


                           SLUG

        (As Ms. Guerrero)
Eros harrows my heart:
wild gales sweeping desolate
mountains,
uprooting oaks.

### TIM'S SOUL

Susie moans with pleasure, pain and wonder. Her nails dig in and skate across my back. The wounds resemble Chinese calligraphy. Blood stains the sheets. Mine and hers.

(Beat.)

Ten months later, Christmas day. The cold, sterile light of the hospital. Michel screams—just like I did—as he's pulled through a slit in Susie's side.

### SLUG

... 2 ...

### TIM'S SOUL

Life moves so fast. Too fucking fast. One minute, I'm twenty-years-old, banging on the drums. The world is mine. My son's learning to speak. His first word:

### TIM

(As Son)
Dad?

### TIM'S SOUL

The most beautiful music I've ever heard. The following birthday. Cake, candles, gifts, singing. His first sentence:

### TIM

(As Son)
Happy birthday, Dad! I love you ...

### TIM'S SOUL

Each word hits me right in the heart. My work as a drummer is to decipher his word music into drum-beats. I move to that beat every day, while at work, in line at the grocery store, standing before the stove, cooking. Another birthday, ten years later:

SLUG

(As Susie)
Happy birthday, Tim.

TIM'S SOUL

Thirty candles on the cake. No more gifts. We're broke. We argue about money. But we've got one thing that can't be bought: Love.

SLUG

(As Susie)
We both love you. No matter what happens, as long as you're here, we'll be all right.

TIM'S SOUL

Michel sleeps in the next room. He sleeps through anything, thank God. Susie sleeps next to me, no touching. We argued tonight. About money. I was angry when I fell asleep. Still, she whispered into my ear:

SLUG

(As Susie)
No matter what happens, as long as you're here, we'll be all right. We love you.

TIM AND TIM'S SOUL

I love you, too. I'm not going anywhere.

SLUG

... 1 ... Contact.

(The SLUG connects with TIM's head.)

I pierce your flesh, break through your skull, and enter into your brain. I can see little pulses of electricity throbbing around me, like flashes of lightning, lighting

SLUG (con't)

up the night. For a split second—which is, like, an eternity for me—I can see all of those things you see: the birthdays, the boners, the people who look at you with love and need in their eyes. Though I have no emotions, a shudder passes through me.

(Shudders, beat.)

And then everything goes dark.

TIM'S SOUL

What happens when a man dies? I don't know. My mom used to say that I'd be fortunate to die in my sleep. This probably isn't what she had in mind.

(Beat.)

What happens when a man dies? Where does his soul go? I spent a lot of time wrestling with that question while Tim slept. Contrary to popular belief, I don't have an answer for you. But I'm about to find out. Don't move. I'll be right back ...

(Blackout.)

**END OF PLAY**

# Solo Playwriting: An Exercise on Magical Realism

1. Go people-watching. More accurately, go people-listening. Write down snippets of what you hear (for example, names, places, words).
2. Looking at the list you have, think of at least three characters that might use the heard items. These characters could be people, plants, animals, whatever seems right for the snippets on your list.
3. Looking at the phrases on your list, what sort of event from your daily life might evoke you to say one of these things? This is where your play starts.
4. Choose one of your favorite magazines, preferably in print and not digital. Open the magazine to any page, close your eyes, and randomly point. What is the nearest image? This is your setting.
5. Given your characters, starting point, and setting, what would be something that might seem out of place (for example, snow in the living room)? This is the "magical" element that your characters will accept as normal.
6. Take five minutes and free-write as much as you can, making sure there are the elements of Magic Realism present. Swap with someone, and share your thoughts after reading each other's piece.

# For Further Research

Arellano, Jerónimo. *Magical Realism and the History of the Emotions in Latin America.* Lanham, PA: Bucknell University Press, 2015.

Danow, David K. *The Spirit of Carnival: Magical Realism and the Grotesque.* Lexington: University of Kentucky Press, 1995.

Kirby, Michael, and Victoria Nes Kirby, eds. *Futurist Performance.* New York: PAJ Books, 2001.

Parkinson Zamora, Lois, and Wendy B. Faris, eds. *Magical Realism: Theory, History, Community.* Raleigh, NC: Duke University Press, 1995.

The Neo-Futurists. *100 Neo-Futurist Plays: From Too Much Light Makes the Baby Go Blind (30 Plays in 60 Minutes).* Chicago: Neo-Futurists, 2011.

# CHAPTER 9

# Greg Aldrich

PLAYWRIGHT

## *THE RIDICULOUSLY SWEET DREAM APARTMENT*

©2012 Greg Aldrich

### PRODUCTION HISTORY

"The Ridiculously Sweet Dream Apartment" was a national Kennedy Center American College Theatre Festival (KCACTF) finalist in 2013, and it was performed for approximately 300 high-school students at Southern Illinois University Carbondale's 2015 Drama Daze, directed by J. Thomas Kidd.

### CAST OF CHARACTERS
    TONY
    DAVE
    ROB
    MARIA

    SETTING—An apartment. Any City, USA. Present day-ish.

# About the Playwright

Originally from Alaska, Greg Aldrich received his BA from Benedictine College in Atchison, Kansas, and his MFA in Playwriting from Ohio University. He is currently completing his PhD at Southern Illinois University. He is also the author of "Thoughts on Flood Prevention," which is included in this collection.

# Form and Style

"The Ridiculously Sweet Dream Apartment" is one of Greg Aldrich's lighter pieces. It is also one of the few "pure" comedies included in this collection of plays. In fact, "Apartment" exhibits most of the elements inherent in comedy, and its fast-paced timing stretches into the realm of farce. Typically we find something or someone humorous when we relate to the thing or person in one of two ways: (1) we recognize something of ourselves—"I do that! That's just like me!" or (2) we are drawn to the difference between us or our situation and the person or situation we observe—"Ha! Look at them! I am so glad that's not ME!" Characteristics or elements of comedy cut across time and place. We can watch a Japanese **kyogen play** (a short comedy that is inserted among more serious Noh plays) and, even without understanding the language, appreciate the comedy, especially the physical. Comedies are categorized in multiple ways. For example, they might be considered "High," "Low," or "Physical" (or extremely physical, slapstick) versus "Verbal" (humor in the wit of the language). Some say that all comedies derive from **incongruity** (the juxtaposition of unlike things), repetition, or **derision** ("put-down" humor). In addition to these broad characteristics, and regardless of how it is labeled, comedy's key elements include the following:

- **"Rule of Three"**—a specific kind of repetition expressing the idea that a line or an action repeated three times in succession produces a laugh. The first time might be funny, but the audience's expectations rise, and they recognize the joke the second time it occurs, building to a crest of laughter on the third.

166

- Sight gags (visual jokes, like, while perhaps stupid, a rubber chicken!)
- Confusion
- Mistaken identity

Something else vital to comedy is the idea that all ends well by the final line. A topsy-turvy, extraordinary world may be depicted in comedy, but the world rights itself at the play's conclusion. Comedies are integrative and regenerative: outsiders rejoin society; couples marry; all is well with the world. Additionally, at least since the fifth-century BCE Greek dramatist Aristophanes, comedies are grounded in a premise, in a "Happy Idea" that might be formulated as a question: "Wouldn't it be nice if _____?". For example, the Happy Idea for Neil Simon's *The Odd Couple* (discussed briefly in "For Further Study") might be put this way: "Wouldn't it be nice if an extreme slob and a 'neatnik' could coexist happily as roommates?" Comedies work like "well-oiled machines" and should give the effect of effortlessness. By no means, despite its often physical humor, should comedy be considered a lesser form than tragedy or drama. Comedy is difficult to write and equally challenging to direct and perform.

"The Ridiculously Sweet Dream Apartment" uses many of the above elements to induce laughter. Aldrich contemporizes the play through his clever use of cell phones and texting that adds to the confusion. He also includes a letter, a well-worn theatrical convention that precipitates confusion in many earlier plays. Much of this play is bordering on a type of comedy called farce. **Farce** is an extreme form of comedy that moves at a rapid pace; it often employs multiple doors that the characters hide behind and pop in and out of with superb comic timing. Farce also often utilizes physical comedy, like a character flipping over a couch. In fact, you could think of farce as "comedy on steroids." In this case, Aldrich casts "Apartment" in the form of Realism. Like "Supernova," "Fireworks," and other plays in this anthology that are identified as Theatrical Realism, "Apartment" includes recognizable characters with whom we can identify, dialogue to which we can relate, and furniture and props that emulate the real world and are in no way exaggerated or distorted.

# Plays for Further Study

Neil Simon's *The Odd Couple* (1965) fits with a study of "Apartment" because, like Aldrich's comedy, at its root lies the ever-funny juxtaposition of an extremely neat and orderly character with a complete slob (in "Apartment," however, Rob is only pretending to be messy). *The Odd Couple* is also cast in the form of Theatrical Realism; the setting is Oscar Madison's messy house, into which Felix Unger moves after a divorce. A series of incidents transpire, including the hapless double date the men go on with the minor characters of the Pidgeon sisters. While based on complications that arise from the situation of roommates with opposing temperaments, like all of Neil Simon's plays—too often wrongly criticized as simple—the piece runs like clockwork and at its heart are truths about the human condition.

Michael Frayn's madcap *Noises Off* (1982) is a British farce that concerns the offstage and onstage antics of actors who are performing together in a play. While **representational** (envisioned to represent or depict reality), the play's set contributes to the comedy through design by alternating locations (generally on a turntable). Much of the humor derives from the repetition of stage actions and lines as the fictional characters lose their places and forget their blocking while rehearsing the play-within-in-a-play, a low comic farce entitled *Nothing On*. An extended comic bit involves a stage prop: a plate of sardines that must be passed from character to character with split-second timing. Farcical doors enhance the set.

The works of British playwright Alan Ayckbourn, including his play *Bedroom Farce*, would also prove fruitful as companions to "Apartment." Also worth considering are the shorter plays of David Ives included in *All in the Timing: Six One-Act Comedies*—especially "Sure Thing," in which a bell signals a re-start of stage action each time one of the couple says the wrong thing. The theatrical convention of the bell surpasses the Rule of Three as an illustration of the heights to which comic repetition can go.

## CAUTION

Professionals and amateurs are hereby notified that all plays are under copyright and permission must be obtained to use them in any manner. All rights, including professional and amateur stage rights, motion picture, recitation, lecturing, public reading, radio broadcasting, television, video or sound recording, all other forms

# THE RIDICULOUSLY SWEET DREAM APARTMENT

CAST OF CHARACTERS

TONY—A male homosexual in his early twenties. Uptight, neurotic, and compulsive. He's a true romantic at his marshmallowy center.

DAVE—A male heterosexual in his early twenties. Tony's best friend. A cool demeanor hides a melodramatic and romantic soul.

ROB—A male homosexual in his early twenties. Tony and Dave's new roommate.

MARIA—A female in her early twenties. Dave's long-time girlfriend. Overtly in charge of her feminine wiles, Maria is a purposed individual with melodramatic tendencies and flair.

SETTING—An apartment. Any City, USA. Present day-ish.

> **AT RISE:** A living room of a pretty nice apartment with beautiful bay windows. A front door is prominently displayed. Three doors denote bedrooms. One for ROB, one for DAVE, and one for TONY. A hallway leads into a kitchen. The apartment is cluttered with clothing strewn about, haphazardly. TONY talks into a cellphone as HE uses a pair of tongs to manipulate the articles of clothing into a garbage bag.

TONY

(Into the phone)

Oh no, the apartment is great. No, it's great. It's a dream, we love it, we really do. Uh-huh. Yep. That's what I said. It's ridiculously sweet. Great location, great view of the city skyline. There is nothing I could want more in an apartment. In a living space. Not a gosh darn thing, Mom. Quite frankly I'd pay more for the place. Well I got

TONY (con't)
one thousand thirty-three dollars and thirty-six cents left in my bank account
and I would put it all down for a place such as this. One thousand. Thirty-three.
And thirty-six cents, yes. Right now. Pay more. I would. Yes, I thanked your friend
Linda for the sublet. Every time I see her, yes. For this ... trial period. The past
month has been some sort of dream, the guys ... love the place.

(ROB enters swiftly moving towards the bedroom.)

ROB
Those undies are clean, you know.

TONY
Hey, Rob, Rob, Rob, could you—

(The bedroom door closes with a slam.)

Jimminey Christmas.

(Into the phone.)

What? No, Mom, things are just great. Dave loves the place. And the new guy?
Yeah, er ... Rob.

ROB (O.S.)
Robbie!

TONY
(Into the phone)
Yeah, Mom, I don't know. It's a great place, but ...

(ROB enters in a flourish, brandishing even more laundry.)

ROB
Laundry day! Think fast!

TONY

Dude, don't toss your freaking laundry at me. Just look at this place.

ROB

(Checking an imaginary watch)
Oooo, I'm late for flag football practice.

TONY

Dude.

ROB

I'll pick it up later, Neat Nelly. Hey you got all the space with the master bedroom. Two, count them, two, walk-in closets. Until I get a dresser or something I don't have anywhere to put my things.

TONY

And when will that be?

ROB

Oooo, look at the time: flag football.

TONY

Rob!

ROB

(Exiting)
Maybe next week, bro.

TONY

That won't be soon enough!

(ROB exits.)

TONY (con't)

Christ-sicle.

(Into the phone.)

What, Mom? No, I … Yeah, okay, where did this guy Rob come from? How does he know Linda? A friend of a friend of a … Just because he's gay as well—you know, Mom, not all men who like men are the same. That's gaycism, Mother—Well, he leaves his clothes everywhere. Well, he says he doesn't have enough closet space. He's got to go. I'm going to lose my thought making space.

(There's a knock at the front door. TONY continues to speak into the phone.)

Look I gotta go. Could you say something to Linda please? I'd like sole control of the lease here. One thousand and thirty-three dollars. And thirty-six cents, yes. Mom, if I could find someone else to stay here we wouldn't have taken him on in the first place—

(Violent, unceasing knocking.)

One second.

(HE answers the door. MARIA is there.)

MARIA

Hi-ya, Tony.

TONY

Maria, hey, Dave said you might come by, but he's not here. Sorry—

MARIA

I just got back into the city last night, settled in, and I wanted to come by and see you guys's new place.

TONY

Ta-da.

MARIA

And maybe we could talk for a sec? I brought cook-ies.

TONY

(Into phone)
What, Ma? No, I gotta go. Kisses, sure.

(To MARIA.)

Okay, just, sure, just make yourself at home. That's great.

MARIA

The kids were terrors this year at camp—hm.

TONY

(Beaming)
Take it in, girl.

MARIA

Did a bomb go off?

TONY

But your *place* is so much better?

MARIA

It's neater.

                         TONY
But the place?

                         MARIA
This is definitely a great location.

                         TONY
Maria ...

                         MARIA
    (Winking)
Well, I can't really see it under all these clothes everywhere, now can I?

                         TONY
Don't set your purse down. You'll lose it in this sea.

                         MARIA
What's eating your face off?

                         TONY
I gotta get rid of this roommate from hell. I've been pushed up against the brink.
Nothing is sacred with this guy.

                         MARIA
Come on, after a month?

                         TONY
When you know, you know. And a month is enough time, believe me. Something
must be done. First off, he is systematically destroying my dating life.

                         MARIA
Oooo, there's a boy? Tell me about him.

TONY

We're just talking, past couple months.

MARIA

An online thing?

TONY

There's nothing shady about that—sixty-two percent of romances starts online nowadays.

MARIA

You just made that statistic up, huh?

TONY

Only sixty-two percent of it. But "Couple Match Forever" has staggering success rates.

MARIA

You even know what this guy looks like?

TONY

That's half the fun of dating on the internet. But they could always fake it anyway, so why bother. Find out in person. I didn't even put up a picture.

MARIA

You're a weirdo.

TONY

Neither did he. He's a ...

MARIA

weirdo.

TONY

You and Dave didn't need the "Couple Match Forever," good for you. But for the rest of us who don't run into the love of our lives in our everyday lives, we have to find our love in all sorts of unexpected places.

MARIA

Oh my, did you just use the L-word?

TONY

I did not.

MARIA

Oooo, someone is crushing hard ...

TONY

Maybe, but I can't really go out with him, because every time I ask him out, this Rob guy trashes the apartment and I have to cancel with this great guy. Like tonight. And my feelings are serious this time.

MARIA

Oh yeah?

TONY

A hunch. But just look at this place.

MARIA

I get it.

TONY

I don't think that you do. Here let me see your purse. Here's some underwear lying around ...

MARIA

Don't put that in my purse!

TONY

Now you get to see what it's like for another person's clothes to invade your personal space.

MARIA

Hey, hey, hey, I get it.

TONY

I don't think you do. Leave it there until you get it.

MARIA

Well, if you've already signed the lease, I'm not sure what you plan to do.

TONY

Ah-ha! It's a trial period, prove we're not dirty men-child—

MARIA

Men are heathens.

TONY

(Gesturing to the apartment)
This Rob animal is!

MARIA

(With a shrug)
More messy than dirty, really.

TONY

Look, this week we sign the lease for the full year. Or we're out on our tushies, but look at this place! Something has to be done. I'd pay more to get sole rights to that lease. But we'd still need a third roommate. And I stupid love this dream apartment.

MARIA

You know, I gotta cousin who's looking for a place.

TONY

In the city?

MARIA

He isn't getting along with one of his roommates and is looking for a new situation. Something with more closet space. My cousin is like ridiculously neat. OCD-like. Has to have a place for everything. Folds his shirts with like 12 folds. Like this.

(SHE demonstrates with a piece of clothing.)

TONY

Is he single?

MARIA

What about your—

TONY

*Kidding*. It'd be a dream to live with someone that neat. I gotta sell that boyfriend of yours on my plan, though the two have gotten kind of chummy in the past couple weeks …

MARIA

I think he's going to break-up with me.

TONY

Where's that coming from?

MARIA

Women's intuition.

TONY

No way.

MARIA

He's been talking about getting me alone to "talk" for like the last week. All of a sudden.

TONY

Maybe he's waiting to pop the question.

MARIA

No way. I know him. New apartment. New life. New girlfriend. He just doesn't want to be around his friends when he does it, because he's afraid of what they would say. Taking sides.

TONY

Yeah, no, I'm not gonna *take* sides—

MARIA

Out with the old, in with the new, but *I'm* not having it.

TONY

Surely, you are going to have to be alone with him sometime? I mean, logistically speaking, right?

MARIA

Not until he comes back to his senses and realizes that I am the only possible woman for him.

TONY

Okay …

MARIA

I'm gonna get him dependent on me again.

TONY

That sounds healthy.

MARIA

Tony.

TONY

That sounds like some sort of some-a-mah-thing.

MARIA

So you'll help me?

TONY

You're seriously gonna lose that purse if you leave it adrift in this ocean of clothes.

MARIA

I'll remember where I put it, *Mom*. I'm not gonna leave without my purse.

TONY

Dave's my friend, it's my job to look out for him.

MARIA

I'll get my cousin to sign the lease with your mother's friend if you help me with this.

TONY

Of course this is in his best interest. Being with you. Getting rid of this bad influence in my—*his*—life. Come to think of it, Rob might be the person behind all this breaking up talk. So *you* gotta help *me*.

MARIA

You just have to keep me from being alone with Dave. And he'll be around me and feel all my feminine charms and realize what a big mistake he's making.

TONY

Nothing easier.

(The door opens and DAVE enters with a giant box.)

MARIA

Dave! Honey!

DAVE

Hey … You … Sweetheart …

MARIA

It's good to see you.

DAVE

Been a long, interesting summer—How were the terrors?

MARIA

What's in the box?

DAVE

… stuff. Nothing interesting.

MARIA

Kiss?

DAVE

Let me just put this in my room.

MARIA

A teensy one.

    (HE juggles the box away from MARIA and gives her a quick teensy one and
    quickly moves away with his box.)

On the cheek?

DAVE

In front of company?

TONY

Don't mind me, I'll just go—I mean, mind me, this is my space too. Ew, too
much PDA, I can't take it, like radiation. Eating at my ... speaking responses.

DAVE

See honey?

MARIA

I'm sure that's not what he meant at all.

TONY

I don't know what I'm saying.

MARIA

You like to watch—*don't* you?

TONY

Oh, yeah, right, sure, exactly. I love it. Get me some popcorn with extra butter. Or
where are those cookies. Mm-mm.

    (DAVE manages to get to the door to his room. Quickly stashes the box
    inside.)

DAVE

Alright everybody—is there, like, some inside joke I'm not privy to here?

TONY

Maria's got a lead on a new roommate.

DAVE

We're looking for a new roommate?

TONY

Dude, come on. This isn't a surprise. Look around.

MARIA

It'd really help me out.

DAVE

What's Rob going to do?

TONY

Whatever he wants. It'll be much like now. Except he won't be living here.

DAVE

Tony could you give me and Maria a moment to talk?

TONY

Ooo ...

MARIA

Actually, I'm just about to head off.

DAVE

I thought maybe we could talk. I haven't seen you all summer—

MARIA

Can't. Places to go. People to see.

DAVE

Like who?

MARIA

My cousin. I should meet with him. About all this. He's staying in the neighbor-hood. I'm gonna go call him. Ta ta for now!

DAVE

Wait, honey.

(SHE exits swiftly without her purse.)

That was … weird.

TONY

No idea what you're talking about there. That verbal exchange was completely normal in every sense of the words fitting together-like.

DAVE

Hey, I need the apartment tonight.

TONY

Um, okay.

DAVE

I gotta talk with Maria. Like alone. It's serious.

TONY

Uh-huh.

DAVE

Yeah.

TONY

Well, I certainly don't want to get in the middle of that.

DAVE

Um. I would hope not.

TONY

So you should take it out of here. Away from me. And my involvement.

DAVE

No, this is the perfect place for it. The beginning of my new … New apartment, new life, new—Well, out with the old. Though we should pick the place up a bit, huh?

TONY

I'm in the process of picking it up. For good.

DAVE

It's still the adjustment period. The sublet trial. Now, the apartment …

TONY

No can do, I gotta date tonight myself. The one I've been putting off for weeks because of the living-sitch.

DAVE

And you were going to tell me when?

TONY

When I got this dump picked up. Look, I'm telling you now.

                                    DAVE

And Rob ... ?

                                    TONY

I don't care about Rob.

                                    DAVE

You don't know him. You've barely spoken to the guy in the past month. You never call him to do anything.

                                    TONY

Hey, I don't even have his number. When you know, you know.

                                    DAVE

Come on, Dude.

                                    TONY

Dave, we've been friends a long time: what's it going to take for you to get onboard with this?

                                    DAVE

The apartment. Tonight.

                                    TONY

And you'll agree to look at Maria's cousin?

                                    DAVE

A deal?

                                    TONY

What's one more night. My man! But put it in writing? What? Write Rob a note saying it's over.

                              DAVE

Um ... okay.


                              TONY

Pen. Paper. Here you go.


                              DAVE
        (Writing)
We've had good times, but, I'm sorry. It's not working out. I hate to be the
bearer of bad news. But there are plenty of other fish in the sea. Particularly in
a city like this. Cheers.

        (TONY's phone rings. TONY looks at it.)


Dude aren't you going to answer that?


                              TONY

Wouldn't miss it ...

        (Into the phone.)


Yep. Nope. Still here-ish.


                              DAVE

That Maria?


                              TONY
        (Into the phone)
Yeah, well, I am in the middle of—Not now, I'm—Yeah, sure the deal—


                              DAVE

It is Maria, bro—

TONY

(Into the phone)
What? Meet your cousin at the coffee shop around the corner? That's inconceivably sudden, and yet amazingly convenient.

DAVE

Dude, let me talk to her, for a sec.

TONY

(Into the phone)
You're breaking up! Bad connection! I'll be by in a sec—
Okay bye.

DAVE

Dude.

TONY

Oops, lost her. Well, I'll see you in a bit.

DAVE

Hey, I'll go with you. I should meet this guy.

TONY

You gotta pick up the place. For tonight.

DAVE

Dude.

TONY

I pass the tongs to you.

(TONY hands off the tongs. Exits.)

DAVE

(Taking in the apartment)

Shit.

(DAVE picks up a tong-full of clothes, questioningly. Smells it. Tentatively.)

Well, that's a relief.

(ROB enters.)

ROB

Just saw Tony leave. Had to duck him because of my flag football excuse.

DAVE

Rob, glad you're here, bro. Maria's back in the city.

ROB

You propose already?

DAVE

I couldn't get her alone. But I got Tony to leave me the apartment tonight.

ROB

Good for you, man. This Mary chick sounds awesome.

DAVE

(Lost in the stars)

Ma-ri- Oh, hey, need your help, bro.

ROB

You're helping me with my problem, right? We got "Operation Master Bedroom" underway.

DAVE

I thought we were going with "Operation Laundry Everywhere"?

ROB

Whichever.

DAVE

About that—Tony wants to bring in a new roommate.

ROB

Another roommate? Where would they stay?

DAVE

Your room?

ROB

And I'd finally get the master bedroom, nice—Wait, where would Tony stay?

DAVE

He'd still be in the master bedroom.

ROB

Oh shit.

DAVE

He even had me write you this note.

ROB

"It's not working out … Other fish in the sea … Cheers?" That's cold, bro.

DAVE

I thought that last bit was clever. 'Cause it sounds likea "break-up, break-up" letter.

ROB

There's no name on it.

DAVE

Well, I wasn't actually planning on leaving it for you, Dude.

ROB

Shit.

DAVE

So maybe you could just chill for a little bit, keep things on the DL. We'll figure out the room situation down the line.

ROB

That peanut sized room is too small. I can't live there. There's no closet space. I can't bring a boy over to that hole. I've been having that online thing on Couple Match Forever for three months now, but I can't begin to go out with him, because what if the conversation turned to, "Well, why don't we go to your place?" It'd be a joke. Dude would probably die laughing.

DAVE

Would you?

ROB

He's the one, Dude. I can't take that chance.

DAVE

Oh yeah?

ROB

This hunch. But it's driving me bat-crap crazy to act this messy. I feel my skin crawl whenever I see sock in a ball.

DAVE

Well, it would be kind of dope if you would get this place picked up for my thing tonight with Maria.

ROB

Oh thank God, yes.

(ROB begins to meticulously pick up the clothes and intricately folds them with 12 folds. Stops.)

Maybe I could even iron?

DAVE

It's gotta be messy again tomorrow.

ROB

(Sighing and continuing)
Right, right. We could get our own place. The two of us. Just saying.

DAVE

He's my best friend—*Oh*, the favor.

ROB

Yep.

DAVE

You gotta get your mom—

ROB

Hold up, text message. No way, the dude's canceling *again*. Shit, I'm never going to meet this guy. You know what? Forget it. No, *no*, no: he can't cancel on me again.

DAVE

I thought he was "the one"?

ROB

(Texting)

Even "the one" has limits. I'm gonna give him a piece of my mind—

DAVE

Let him have it.

ROB

I will. He'll learn not to "play" me.

DAVE

Amen, brother. Ha.

ROB

Sent.

DAVE

And if he comes to his sense?

ROB

Oh god, yes—you think he will?

DAVE

Well, there you go. Ah, favor.

ROB

What's up, Dude?

DAVE

You gotta talk to this lady, Linda. Your mom knows her, right?

                              ROB
Yeah, why?


                              DAVE
She just called me. Apparently she's found some other interested party in living here.


                              ROB
Oo.


                              DAVE
And is thinking about voiding the sublet trial.


                              ROB
Were you a dick to her?


                              DAVE
What? No. I was just seeing if I could put off my share of the rent …


                              ROB
Uh-huh.


                              DAVE
Jeez Dude, rings and things cost money!


                              ROB
What sorta things?


                              DAVE
So if you could call her or your mom or something, it'd be great, 'cause I don't want to lose this place.

ROB

No worries man. I got the lease right here. She made it out last week: we just gotta sign.

DAVE

Ah-ha! This is why she was so anxious!

ROB

I already signed it. You do the same and when Tony signs it we'll be golden.

DAVE

Sweet.

(HE signs.)

There you go.

ROB

Oooo, wait, text.

(Checking it.)

Okay, maybe this guy's coming around.

DAVE

I told you it all works out.

ROB

He'll meet. He said to give him a moment to sort some business out at his place.

DAVE

Well, I gotta get some things to prepare for tonight.

|                          ROB | DAVE |
|---|---|
| Candles? | Wouldn't you like to know ... |
| Champagne? | Kidding, yes, you're right, it's |
| Edible *undies*— | only champagne. |

DAVE

No.

ROB

In your room?

DAVE

No.

ROB

Let me see—Ooo, another text.

DAVE

Work it.

ROB

Just my cousin. She's in the area. She can come by?

DAVE

No, I need the place tonight, remember?

ROB

Cool, cool. I'll see if we can meet up later.

DAVE

Ah, Maria's purse.

>                                    ROB
>          (Still texting)
> Oo, never mess with a woman's purse man.

>                                    DAVE
> We don't have secrets like that.

>                                    ROB
> Temptations got to be like ri-dic to look in it, right?

>                                    DAVE
> No. Not at all. Not till you said something.

>                                    ROB
>          My bad.

>                                    DAVE
> Look, I gotta jet, if I'm going to have everything ready in time.

>                                    ROB
> I'm gonna put these clothes away. For now. Le sigh.

>          (Holding up an article of clothing.)

> I mean look at this: I wouldn't even recognize this as my own it's so wrinkly.

>          (DAVE looks at the purse in his hands and sets it down. Goes to the door.
>          Runs back and grabs it close to his chest.)

>                                    DAVE
>          (To justify)
> In case I see her.

(HE exits out the front, swiftly. ROB gathers the remainder of the clothes and takes them into his bedroom. TONY bursts in the front door.)

TONY

Dave? Dave you around? We gotta talk about tonight. Something's come up. Shit. What's this paper? Motherbleepers signed the lease. That backstabbing …

(There's a knock at the door.)

Christ.

(HE answers. MARIA comes in.)

I told you to wait downstairs.

MARIA

Dave here?

TONY

The dude is screwing me. He totally said we'd get your cousin in here and now he's already signed the lease with his new pal-y-pal Rob.

MARIA

I just came to get my purse. Wait, where is my purse?

TONY

I told you not to set it adrift.

MARIA

Shit.

                    TONY
Fuck Dave, man.

                    MARIA
Careful. Ooo, text. Goddamn it, Dave. You can stick around tonight?

                    TONY
You know what? I got it.

                    MARIA
Got what?

                    TONY
A plan. You need Dave to be dependent on you?

                    MARIA
Yeah, then he won't get away.

                    TONY
We'll get a new lease—your cousin have like a friend or something, that he might be able to move in as well?

                    MARIA
But Dave ... ?

                    TONY
Then he'll have to, like, crash with you. He'll be utterly dependent on you.

                    MARIA
I'll check ... Here. Short text ...

                    TONY
There's just enough time to run upstairs and talk to Linda—get a new copy of the lease.

                              MARIA
If she's home.


                              TONY
Don't be a negative Nelly.


                              MARIA
Text. Oooo, he says he does have someone that's a possible candidate.


                              TONY
This is gonna work out. It's got to.


                              MARIA
Uh-huh.

        (TONY's phone rings.)


                              TONY
Mom? Oh my god, you won't believe what's happened—

        (TONY exits. MARIA paces the space. Spots the note.)


                              MARIA
Hm, a note. Dave's handwriting … "Good times … ", "but … ",
"fish … ", "sea … " Oh, god. It's happening. It's really happening. Starting not to
breathe. Oh, god …

        (The sound of DAVE muttering to himself in a panic.)

Oh, god. I gotta hide … Kitchen!

        (MARIA ducks into the kitchen just as DAVE enters into the apartment.)

                              DAVE

Rob! Robbie!

        (ROB enters.)

                              ROB

What, Dude?

                              DAVE

You won't believe this sitch. I know why Maria won't be alone with me. There's another dude!

                              ROB

No way.

                              DAVE

Check it, I found another man's briefs in her purse.

                              ROB

Aw crapstick man. Told you not to look.

                              DAVE

I don't know what I'm gonna do. I can't breathe. Shoot. Aw, chalk me sideways, man.

                              ROB

There there, Dude.

                              DAVE

If I see her I'm gonna completely lose it. I can't believe she'd do this to me.

                              ROB

Look we'll figure this out.

DAVE

I can't even look at this place, man. Everything reminds me of her. These clothes, this wall … aw, man this wall!

ROB

Um … you just moved here.

DAVE

But she's my life, her electrons penetrate everything, every object I come in contact with. Oh, god. I gotta close my eyes.

ROB

Hey look, I know this place is ridiculously sweet and all, but my cousin found this place where you and I could move in.

DAVE

What about Tony?

ROB

He'll figure his shit out. This is a great place. Other dudes will want in.

DAVE

I changed my mind: I want to live here forever. Then I'll always be surrounded by her.

ROB

Okay …

DAVE

My throat is closing up—

ROB

Just breathe man. Onnnnneeee. Twwwwwooooo. Thrrrrrreeeeeee.

(TONY enters.)

TONY

Hey she wasn't—Ah-ha! Just look what we have here.

ROB

Shhh!

TONY

Naw, no "shhhhhhhhhhhhhhhhhhhhhhh," bro. Hey there *roommies*.

ROB

Easy, Tony. Dave's had a shock.

TONY

No, you know who's had a shock? Me, that's who. Look what I discovered.

(HE brandishes the signed lease.)

ROB

Yeah, I got the lease. You just have to sign—then the apartment is ours.

TONY

It's like that is it? Don't think I don't know what's going on here. I see your little game. But you know what? This is what I think of your little contract. Fffffff-shick.

(HE tears the lease in half.)

ROB

You didn't!

TONY

Oh yes I did.

ROB

That was our only copy of the lease!

TONY

I'll get another. And then your goose will be cooked.

ROB

She has another renter! Now none of us get the apartment.

TONY

Shit, what?

ROB

You just f'd us.

TONY

Well, if you didn't just leave your clothes all around!

ROB

If you hadn't stolen the master bedroom!

TONY

Woah, what, hold on.

ROB

I called dibsies.

TONY

You're the new guy to the trio. You don't get to "call" anything.

ROB

Well, it's not gonna be a trio. I've gotta a lead on a new even more ridiculously sweet dream apartment from my cousin. I'm calling her right now. And there's just room for two. Count it. One. Two. So there.

DAVE

Oh god, no. I need to be here. Where she was. Briefly. Ever so brief.

ROB

And I'm sorry about that.

(ROB dials. A phone rings from the kitchen. THEY all look over. ROB goes into the kitchen.)

Maria ... ? Cuz ... ?

(ROB enters with MARIA sobbing.)

MARIA

No, I can't look at him.

ROB

Wait, what?

TONY

No freaking way. This is your cousin?

MARIA

Uh-huh.

ROB

And you guys are ... ? Were.

ROB (con't)

This is phenomenally coincidental.

TONY

(To ROB)

You know that even more ridiculously sweet apartment you were just banking on ...

ROB

*No.*

TONY

Yep.

ROB

Shit.

TONY

So I guess this is the end for everybody. We didn't sign the lease and we all have to leave. Tomorrow.

ROB

All because you wouldn't give up the master bedroom.

TONY

What? You want more space to be a mess in?

ROB

(Sincerely)

For the record, I'm a very neat person. Meticulously neat. It's been hell trying to keep things messy enough that you'd give me the master bedroom. I just needed more closet space. Shit, I'm sorry if I pushed you.

TONY

Look if you just wanted more closet space … I could've given you one of my closets to store stuff.

ROB

Too late now.

TONY

Seems I don't know you as well as I thought I did.

ROB

Yeah.

DAVE

Maria.

MARIA

Yes, Dave?

DAVE

I'm sorry it's come to this.

MARIA

Me too.

(A long moment.)

DAVE

Wait, why are you upset?

MARIA

Um, your letter.

                    DAVE

What letter?

                    MARIA

Here.

                    TONY

This was for Rob.

                    MARIA

What?

                    ROB

Oh god, this has all been a huge misunderstanding.

                    DAVE

But the briefs?

    (DAVE presents them again. ROB snatches them.)

                    ROB

Those darn wrinkles!

                    TONY

Whoops. I. Some kind of misguided lesson about personal space ...

                    MARIA

Oh Dave!

                    DAVE

Maria!

    (THEY go to each other. Passionately.)

TONY

Um, get a room.

ROB

While you still can. Before the money takes over.

TONY

What money?

DAVE

Some dude offered Linda another thousand and thirty-three dollars and thirty-six cents to get the apartment.

TONY

A thousand and thirty-three dollars and thirty-six cents?

DAVE

For the lease.

TONY

That was me, I offered her a thousand and thirty-three dollars and thirty-six cents for control of the lease.

DAVE

So it's still ours?

TONY

Well, mine. Technically.

ROB

And what about me?

DAVE

Come on, Tony.

TONY

You're really *neat*? Really, *really* neat?

MARIA

Meticulously. Perhaps too meticulously.

ROB

No such thing.

MARIA

Don't be too sure.

TONY

You can stay. On a trial basis. And I'll even give you one of the closets.

DAVE

(To MARIA)

Should we ... get that room? I had some things I wanted to show you.

(ROB chuckles. DAVE gives him a not now look. A moment. TONY and ROB sit on the couch.)

TONY

Oh shit, I totally spaced my date.

ROB

No, shit, me too.

                              TONY
I'll just text him …

        (ROB's and TONY's phones beep simultaneously.)

                              ROB
Uh …

                              TONY
No …

                              ROB
Anthony?

                              TONY
Roberto??!

                              ROB
No shit. We really have no idea who the other one is, do we?

                              TONY
When you don't know, you don't know.

        (A moment.)

                              ROB
Huh.

                              TONY
Huh.

        (A moment.)

TONY (con't)

Well, let's actually go and find out then.

ROB

At least we'll know the apartment is acceptable to come back to.

TONY

You're that sure of yourself.

ROB

A hunch—

(TONY's phone rings. HE looks at it and answers quickly.)

TONY

NoyesuhhuhitallworkedoutfinethankyouMom. Kisses, sure.

(HE hangs up.)

Shall we?

(THEY exit. A moment. A delighted shriek emits from the bedroom.)

MARIA

Yes! Oh my god, yes! Of course I will!

## END OF PLAY

# What's in a Name?: An Exercise on Comedy

1.  Often a play's title is embedded in the dialogue. Who first uses the phrase "ridiculously sweet apartment"? When does this come in the play? How many times is the phrase used and by whom throughout the play?
2.  Review the elements of comedy discussed in the "Form and Style" style section that precedes the script. How many of the elements are displayed in this play? Give specific examples.
3.  Watch a television sitcom and identify elements of comedy. What is the show's premise or Happy Idea?

# For Further Research

Bermel, Albert. *Farce: The Comprehensive and Definitive Account of One of the World's Funniest Art Forms.* New York: Touchstone, 1983.

Romanska, Magda, and Alan Ackerman, eds. *Reader in Comedy: An Anthology of Theory and Criticism.* New York: Bloomsbury Methuen, 2016.

Szakolczai, Arpad. *Comedy and the Public Sphere: The Rebirth of Theatre as Comedy and the Genealogy of the Modern Public Arena.* New York and London: Routledge, 2015.

# CHAPTER 10

# Bradley Stephenson

PLAYWRIGHT

## *REVOLVER*

©2015 Bradley Stephenson

### PRODUCTION HISTORY

Originally written as a full-length play, "Revolver" was adapted by the playwright, specifically for this anthology, into the short form in which it appears here. The original version had a workshop reading at the Missouri Playwrights' Workshop and received a concert reading at the Mizzou New Play Series 2014 (David Crespy, Artistic Director), directed by Drew Darr.

### CAST OF CHARACTERS
    EDIE (EE-dee)
    APRIL
    MARSHALL
    TY

SETTING—A mid-sized college town in the United States. The living room of the shared apartment of the three roommates. Late at night, the night before college graduation. Present day.

## PLAYWRIGHT'S NOTE

Directors are encouraged to make changes to pop culture, song, and celebrity references to keep the play current.

Please make every effort to cast an actress with a real mobility impairment in the role of Edie.

# About the Playwright

Bradley Stephenson is Assistant Professor of Theatre Arts at Catawba College, where he directs and teaches playwriting, acting, script analysis, theatre history, introduction to theatre, and courses in the Honors Program.

He earned his PhD in theatre from the University of Missouri, where his research explored topics from musicals and metatheatre to disability and dramatic criticism. He was the Associate Director of Research for the Center for Applied Theatre and Drama Research at Mizzou, where he also taught classes in acting, playwriting, storytelling, and script analysis. Brad is a director, an actor, and a playwright. His play *Truffles and Nougat* received its world premiere at Talking Horse Theatre in 2016. His scholarly work has been published in *Theatre Topics, Studies in Musical Theatre, Ecumenica, The Journal of American Drama and Theatre,* and *Journal of Dramatic Theory and Criticism.* Dr. Stephenson is also a freelance vocal music arranger with nearly six hundred arrangements to his name (www.acasongs.com).

# Form and Style

"Revolver" is cast in the form of Realism, with recognizable three-dimensional characters and nuanced relationships, dialogue that focuses on "real world," personal issues, and a representational setting. Its **linear action** (cause and effect chain of plot events) does not preclude the implementation of "reveals" or even surprises—what we often call perception shifts.

Stephenson's centering the piece around a character with a disability moves this play into the realm of **social drama** (plays about tough, current social problems), in the tradition established by playwright Henrik Ibsen, who is often called the Father of Realism. In "Revolver," however, the social issue is not an overt cause like human rights or environmental pollution but, rather, a more subtle depiction of how disabilities are viewed, and of how disabled persons self-identify. The play also calls to mind a pressing issue and topic of discussion in the theatre industry regarding casting: namely, casting appropriate actors who possess the same traits as the characters they portray (for example, physical disability, skin color, or age).

The significance of a play's title is always interesting to explore. In the case of "Revolver," the title began as the playwright's challenge to himself, as he states, "to write a play that contains quotes from every Beatles song on their 1966 *Revolver* Album." He continues: "As the play developed, however, the title took on multiple levels of meaning. The wheels on Edie's chair revolve, and she is also struggling with whether or not to fall into the cycle that so many of her childhood friends embraced, staying in their insular small town and raising kids just like their parents. That theme of cycles and breaking cycles is a large part of the play and the relationships within it. The last line of the play starts it all over and leaves us with just as many questions as we began with." The Beatles quotations were dropped, in part due to copyright issues, but, as Stephenson says, "the title still stuck around."

# Plays for Further Study

In his book *Drama, Disability and Education*, Andy Kempe provides an extensive chronology of disabled dramatic characters, tracing the inclusion of characters with disabilities back to Sophocles's portrayal of the blind seer, Tiresias, in *Oedipus Rex*. Among the plays Kempe lists are two classics that work well in tandem with "Revolver": Tennessee Williams's 1944 *The Glass Menagerie* and Mark Medoff's 1979 *Children of a Lesser God*. Of course, William Gibson's realistic drama *The Miracle Worker* (1959), based on the biography of pioneering disabilities advocate Helen Keller, is a fine choice as well.

In *The Glass Menagerie*, we encounter the character of Laura, impossibly shy, with a limp that literally cripples her social interaction, in addition to other psychological and physical differences that go unnamed. Ann M. Fox's chapter on *The Glass Menagerie* in Kristy Johnston's *Disability Theatre and Modern Drama: Recasting Modernism* situates the piece, written by an abled author with an extraordinary sister, historically in the field of disability studies.

Because Williams' play is a hybrid play *The Glass Menagerie* works well in comparison to other plays included in this collection. In fact, one of the play's major concerns as well as a theme expressed in much twentieth-century dramatic literature—truth versus illusion—is mirrored in the production elements the playwright presents. As a "memory play" that incorporates a narrator, *The Glass Menagerie* provides a great compliment to Jacob Juntunen's "The First Yes" as well.

*Children of a Lesser God* tackles the subject of deaf rights and individuals' rights to determine their place in society—choices of whether or not to use American Sign Language (ASL) exclusively, to lip-read, or to speak aloud. The deafness depicted in *Children of a Lesser God* can serve to stand for any manifestation of the extraordinary body seeking fair treatment and a successful life in a predominantly abled society. Like "Revolver," *Children of a Lesser God* is cast in a **realistic** (meaning of or like "the real") form.

## CAUTION

# REVOLVER

## CAST OF CHARACTERS

EDIE (EE-dee)—early 20s, female, roommate, college senior, has been accepted to graduate school in engineering, headstrong but lonely, uses a wheelchair to get around due to a spinal cord injury. If possible, the audience should not be aware of the injury or Edie's disability until her wheelchair is revealed.

APRIL—early 20s, female, roommate, college senior, plus-sized, sexy, brash and overconfident to mask her insecurity, best friends with and very protective of Edie.

MARSHALL—early 20s, male, roommate, college senior, going to Medical school at Johns Hopkins in the fall, overcommitted and conflicted, all-American good looks.

TY—early 20s, male, an observant and philosophical drifter type who doesn't live there but never seems to leave.

SETTING—A mid-sized college town in the United States. The living room of the shared apartment of the three roommates. Late at night, the night before college graduation. Present day.


## PLAYWRIGHT'S NOTE

Directors are encouraged to make changes to pop culture, song, and celebrity references to keep the play current. Please make every effort to cast an actress with a real mobility impairment in the role of Edie.

**AT RISE:** The living room of the apartment shared by EDIE, APRIL, and MARSHALL. There are boxes and suitcases around, perhaps a few empty beer cans and wine bottles. A couch is center with not much else in the way of furniture. Up stage center is the front door as well as a kitchenette with a refrigerator. Stage right is the bathroom door, stage left are the bedrooms, which are on a landing that goes up one step. There is a piece of plywood serving as a makeshift ramp up the step. Outside, there is rain.

It is the night before college graduation. The students are moving out tomorrow after the graduation ceremonies. EDIE is seated on the couch playing solitaire.

Suddenly, APRIL charges in through the front door. SHE is a big, beautiful woman who is wet and angry.

APRIL

I'm so pissed right now, you don't even know.

EDIE

Nice to see you too, April.

APRIL

This top is ruined.

EDIE

I've got some t-shirts I haven't packed yet.

APRIL

I'm not wearing one of your ratty high school t-shirts to my last college party ever, and neither are you.

EDIE

We have to be in line on the quad by eight AM.

APRIL

Nuh uh. No way I'm letting you stay here alone tonight. This top will not be sacrificed in vain. We're getting some action, whether you like it or not.

EDIE

You look like you went swimming. What happened?

APRIL

The moving guys took forever with my stuff and then a thunderstorm came out of nowhere so I had to help get the last boxes in before they all got soaked. This body is not built for manual labor. Although that one mover guy was super cute, didjya see him? Omigod, like Liam Hemsworth.

EDIE

So hot. Looks kinda like a kicked puppy, but in a good way.

APRIL

He's got those eyes that are just deep and wounded and whispering for me to rescue him, you know, but not too wounded that he talks about his mom and like cries while we're making out, but he's gotta act like he doesn't want to be

APRIL (con't)

rescued, but really on the inside his deep, sad, kicked-puppy eyes are just crying out,

(Low, sexy voice.)

"Please, fix me."

EDIE

Unh, take me now!

APRIL

God, I'm gross, I've got to go shower before the party.

EDIE

Hey, I wouldn't go in there right now.

APRIL

That's what the candles are for.

EDIE

No, gross. But you should—

APRIL

Oh! Edie, I almost forgot, your doctor called to confirm your appointment on Tuesday. I said sure.

(APRIL tosses EDIE her cell phone.)

EDIE

April, quit taking my phone!

APRIL

Quit taking my tampons.

EDIE

That was four months ago!

APRIL

Yeah, well.

EDIE

Any other messages? No texts? From Marshall or anybody?

APRIL

Nope, you're still a nerd. I'll be back in a minute.

(APRIL exits to the bathroom.)

EDIE

Or less.

(EDIE picks up the phone and checks it, but there are no new messages. APRIL screams and runs back onstage, covering herself in a towel.)

APRIL

Ahhhhhhhhhh!

EDIE

And there it is.

(TY saunters in from the bathroom. He's a philosophical hippie type and is much more comfortable with his surroundings than he probably should be.)

APRIL

What the hell are you doing in the bathtub, Ty?!

                          TY

Pondering. I like to ponder in the bathroom.


                         APRIL

That's crazy!


                          TY

The tub feels like a cool, porcelain pea pod, reflecting my inner chi.


                         APRIL

You don't live here, you weirdo!


                          TY

I was pondering that, as well.


                         EDIE

Oh, April, can I hang up my gown in the bathroom while you shower to try and
steam out the wrinkles? The creases look awful.


        (EDIE pulls her wheel chair around from behind the couch, revealing it for
        the first time. SHE maneuvers herself into the chair during the following.)


                          TY

Academic regalia, steeped in circumstance and pomp.


                         APRIL

Let me get it for you.


                         EDIE

No, it's cool. I need a break from the sofa, anyway.


                         APRIL

It's right over here, you stay put, I'll get 'em.

                              EDIE

I can get it.


                              APRIL

It's no problem, I need to do mine too.


                              EDIE

Let it go, April.


                              APRIL

I'm just trying to be nice.


                              EDIE

I don't want you to be nice. I want you to be normal.


                              APRIL

Fine. Roll your skinny ass back down the ramp, cause I'm getting the gowns, you weenie.


                              EDIE

Ty, you got yours?


                              TY

The school of life does not have a graduation.


                              EDIE

What?


                              TY

The goodly professor did not appreciate my essay response to her multiple-choice calculus exam.

                                EDIE

How 'bout some Rat Screw, then?


                                 TY

Ah. Egyptian Rat Screw, the game of the pharaohs. A challenge of speed and skill, the heightened awareness of the cards as you anticipate the next play—

        (MARSHALL enters up center, a bit out of breath, and carrying some books and an umbrella.)


                                EDIE

The prodigal son returns.


                              MARSHALL

Hey guys. Hey, Ty.


                               APRIL

Hi, Marshall.


                              MARSHALL

Hey.


                               APRIL

Is it still raining out there?


                              MARSHALL

A little. Looks like the storm's clearing up, though.


                               APRIL

Books? C'mon, Marsh, college is over as of nine AM tomorrow. It is time to let it go.


                              MARSHALL

I know. I've just got this summer research grant I've got to get started on.

APRIL

No med school is worth losing your summer break, and we've got that party over at the Lambda house later. Here, have a beer.

(SHE hands MARSHALL a beer from the fridge.)

MARSHALL

Thanks, but I've really got to get my letter of intent sent in before they cut off our internet.

TY

I'll take a flask of mead.

APRIL

It's beer, you weirdo!

(To MARSHALL.)

Starbucks has free Wi-Fi, you can get it near the window in my room.

EDIE

Nice of you to finally join us.

MARSHALL

Edie, hey.

APRIL

I'm getting in the shower now. You better not be studying when I get out.

(To TY.)

And you better not be pondering, either.

TY

You can't wake a person who is pretending to be asleep.

APRIL

Just go home!

TY

I think she would benefit from a retreat of silent meditation.

APRIL

And you would benefit from a swift kick in the nads!

(SHE advances on him. HE retreats quickly to the door.)

TY

I believe my laundry is now completed, so I shall go sort and fold.

APRIL

Have you been stealing my quarters?!

TY

(With a quick formal bow)
Tzai' huei'! [formal Mandarin for "So long"]

(Exits.)

APRIL

Ugh. Just twelve more hours.

(SHE storms to the bathroom, but then turns back.)

You two play nice while I'm gone, okay?

(SHE exits. An awkward pause.)

EDIE

So where ya been, Marshall?

MARSHALL

Just out doing some research for a grant application.

EDIE

I was starting to think you had already moved out. I've barely seen you in a week.

MARSHALL

Yeah, I've been busy with—

EDIE

With your grant proposal and med school. I know. I pay attention.

MARSHALL

Um, thanks, I guess.

EDIE

It wouldn't kill you to return a text once in a while.

MARSHALL

You didn't get my text? This afternoon?

EDIE

Nope.

MARSHALL

Weird. Must not have gone through.

EDIE

Weird.

MARSHALL

Sorry. I don't really like texting.

(Another awkward silence.)

You want a beer?

EDIE

No thanks.

MARSHALL

Not drinking anymore?

EDIE

Not thirsty.

MARSHALL

You're always thirsty.

EDIE

I found Jesus.

MARSHALL

Really?

EDIE

Yeah, I'm Catholic now. I think it'll help me get a shot with a Kennedy. I heard JFK's grandnephew or something goes to Stanford, too.

MARSHALL

How ambitious.

EDIE

He'll probably just want to use me for my body, though.

MARSHALL

I doubt it.

EDIE

You doubt it?

MARSHALL

No, I mean, no, they're just Catholics, right? Good, moral guys …

EDIE

So now I'm not moral?

MARSHALL

No, of course you are—

EDIE

That no one could fall for somebody like this?

MARSHALL

Stop it, Edie! That's not what I meant and you know it. You're twisting my words.

EDIE

They seem to twist themselves.

MARSHALL

Alright. What did I do? Huh? What is going on?

EDIE

Whatever, it's my fault.

MARSHALL

Quit being so snippy. You sound like your mom.

(Realizing his mistake.)

I'm sorry, I shouldn't have said that.

(Trying to recover.)

All the great thinkers and artists had screwed up families, right? That bodes well for us.

(HE drinks. Beat.)

EDIE

Marshall?

MARSHALL

Yeah?

EDIE

What if I didn't go?

MARSHALL

Go where?

EDIE

Stanford. Grad school. What if I didn't go? What if I just went back to Green-wood and, I don't know, got a job at the Walgreens on Main Street, maybe? Mr. Jessup was always nice to me. I could get an apartment or something and, I don't know, try to be normal for once.

MARSHALL

Are you joking?

EDIE

No one else from back home is moving on. Just settling down and not worrying about all that other stuff. You know Tracy Sanderson is pregnant with her third kid now.

MARSHALL

From middle school? You keep up with her?

EDIE

Facebook.

MARSHALL

Yeah, well, we got out of that sinkhole.

EDIE

Would you go back with me?

    (Pause.)

Back to Greenwood, and—

MARSHALL

I'm going to med school at Hopkins, and you are going to Stanford for engineering.

EDIE

What if I don't want that anymore?

MARSHALL

I don't understand—

                    EDIE

Would you stay with me?

        (Beat.)

                    MARSHALL

Edie ... we're, uh ... we're not together. I mean, we grew up together, and all that, but we're not together ... together.

                    EDIE

I know.

                    MARSHALL

I mean ...

                    EDIE

I just thought since // you—

                    MARSHALL

Yeah, I know. That was ... it just kinda happened.

                    EDIE

Yeah.

                    MARSHALL

I'm glad it did. I mean it's not like I haven't thought about it before, or anything.

                    EDIE

Really?

                    MARSHALL

Yeah, of course. I'm a guy, you're a girl. Guys think about it.

EDIE

How much do you think about it?


MARSHALL

Stop it. I'm just saying … We've got a lot of history, us two. Kinda weird that we haven't done it together sooner, you know?


EDIE

Why's that?


MARSHALL

I don't know, maybe it's not so weird. And it wasn't just a hook up, not to me anyways. I mean … it was special. The formal didn't suck, and you looked great in your dress, with your hair … and I was so proud of you for getting into Stanford, and you were really listening to me, you know, when I was just rambling on about April and all of that drama last semester … You seemed like you enjoyed it, at least I thought you did? So … Like we've been friends for like fifteen years, through your accident and your mom leaving town and all that. And when the whole thing with my dad went down … And then us going to college together? I mean, it's like that night was kinda the perfect send off, right? Now that we're going our separate ways? I don't know what I'm talking about, can you just say something, please?


EDIE

Like what?


MARSHALL

I don't want to mess up our friendship. We've got too much history to throw all that away because of one night, right?


EDIE

Right.

MARSHALL

Right.

(APRIL enters from the bathroom in a robe with a towel wrapped around her hair. SHE notices the tension.)

APRIL

Shoulda guessed you two would have ruined the party.

EDIE

I should go finish packing.

APRIL

You finished last week. You're more prepared than a boy scout.

EDIE

I was a Brownie, thank you.

(EDIE starts to roll towards her bedroom, as APRIL gets two beers.)

MARSHALL

Edie …

EDIE

No, it's fine. I just wanna get my last ducks in a row.

APRIL

Whatever.

MARSHALL

Are you turning in for the night?

                              EDIE
Maybe.

    (EDIE exits.)

                            MARSHALL
Then goodnight. Maybe.

                              APRIL
Do they put awkward in the water wherever you two are from?

                            MARSHALL
Probably.

    (APRIL gives him a beer.)

Thanks.

                              APRIL
You look tired.

    (SHE lounges next to him on the couch.)

                            MARSHALL
It's late.

                              APRIL
Anything going on between you two?

                            MARSHALL
What, me and Edie? No.

APRIL

Why is she texting you so much?

MARSHALL

We're friends, is all. You know we go way back.

APRIL

I don't know. I've got plenty of friends from way back, and we don't text like that. What is she so eager to tell you?

MARSHALL

Are you reading her texts?

APRIL

She's socially inept; I have to make sure she's not making a fool of herself. I'm protecting her, just like you said you were doing.

MARSHALL

She said she never got that text.

APRIL

She's technologically inept, too. Or maybe she just lied.

MARSHALL

That's not like her.

APRIL

She'll be fine. Don't beat yourself up.

(SHE makes herself more comfortable on the couch and swigs the beer.)

You ok? Are things still weird between us?

MARSHALL

What? No, no. That was forever ago.

APRIL

Good. 'Cause I like the way things are now. Nice.

MARSHALL

Yeah.

APRIL

We're moving on.

MARSHALL

We have to be grown ups after tomorrow.

APRIL

Yeah, after tomorrow. But what about tonight? What are we gonna do to celebrate? Ooh! Let's play a truth or dare, high card wins …

MARSHALL

Have you noticed any change in Edie recently? She was acting all weird while you were in the shower.

APRIL

I have no control over what she does while I'm in the shower. I can barely control what I do in the shower …

MARSHALL

No, I mean she seemed a little depressed—

APRIL

That's just her face.

MARSHALL

Has she said anything about me?

APRIL

Maybe you should lay off the texting. Give her some space.

MARSHALL

Really?

APRIL

I mean, the last thing you need right now is a clingy friend from high school making you feel bad about yourself. It'd be good for her, too. Friendships are tough long distance, anyway. Don't get stuck in the past when your future is out there, staring you down, and saying, "Come and take me."

(Pause.)

Anyway, we have a game to play.

MARSHALL

Let's play.

(THEY play.)

APRIL

I win again! Dare, chug your beer.

MARSHALL

Fair enough.

(HE finishes his beer. SHE finishes her beer, too.)

Did you dare yourself, too?

                                APRIL
Kind of. Okay, go.

        (THEY play. MARSHALL wins.)

                            MARSHALL
Alright, my turn. Truth, favorite college memory.

                                APRIL
How boring.

                            MARSHALL
It was a good question.

                                APRIL
The time we hooked up in the library.

                            MARSHALL
Come on.

                                APRIL
I'm serious. I'll remember that forever.

                            MARSHALL
That was awful.

                                APRIL
You didn't think so at the time.

                            MARSHALL
No, I mean in general. In theory. In the grand scheme of stories to tell my
grandkids.

APRIL

I've got a lot of favorite memories that I don't want to tell my grandkids.

MARSHALL

You remember how pissed Edie got?

APRIL

Because you told her! It ruined the whole secret thing we were going for, and then you got all weird, and our special friendship lost its special benefits.

MARSHALL

Maybe we should play another hand?

APRIL

If you say so, Doctor.

(THEY play.)

I win. Dare. Close your eyes.

(Beat.)

MARSHALL

That's not a dare.

APRIL

Sure it is. Close your eyes. It's the rules, you have to do it.

MARSHALL

But I—

APRIL

No buts, just close 'em.

(HE looks at her, knowing what is coming. HE closes his eyes. SHE moves in closer and kisses him. MARSHALL does not pull away. The kissing intensifies. Their bodies press together. Suddenly, TY comes barging in through the front door carrying a loaded laundry basket and singing. APRIL and MARSHALL separate, but not in time.)

TY

I'm a genie in a bottle, you gotta rub me the right way.

(Noticing them on the couch.)

Great Scott! What have we here?

| MARSHALL | APRIL |
|----------|-------|
| Nothing. | Dammit. |

TY

Is that love I smell in the air?

APRIL

Would you quit it?

TY

Nothing like a little late night nookie on the couch, a little pre-commencement canoodling.

MARSHALL

It's not like that.

(EDIE rolls in from off left.)

EDIE

What's going on?

244

MARSHALL

Edie.

APRIL

Crap.

TY

I'm just here to sort and fold, pay no attention to the man behind the laundry.

EDIE

What happened?

TY

What happens in the common room stays in the common room.

EDIE

You said you had stopped.

APRIL

Let me explain, Edie.

EDIE

Are you kidding me?

APRIL

We couldn't help ourselves.

EDIE

You promised me you were done with this. Months ago!

MARSHALL

I am.

APRIL

You promised her?

EDIE

She's messing with your head. I can't keep coming back and rescuing you from your impulses every time some fat slut strokes your ego!

APRIL

What did you just say?

MARSHALL

It was just a kiss.

EDIE

I don't care about the kiss! Kiss whoever you like. Screw whoever you like. Break every heart in the whole damn world! It doesn't matter, you selfish prick!

(SHE lashes out at him physically.)

MARSHALL

Back, off Edie.

(SHE gets in a hit.)

Hey!

TY

Gentle, friends!

APRIL

Get a hold of yourself!

(MARSHALL has escaped and made it up the step to the landing. HE knocks over the plywood ramp so that EDIE cannot follow him.)

                         EDIE

You're worse than your father.

                       MARSHALL

What?!

                         EDIE

The laughing stock of Greenwood, and that's saying a lot ...

        (Continuous.)

                       MARSHALL

Stop it right there ...

                         EDIE

        (Continuous)

You think people just forget about the English teacher who fucks his students? In Greenwood?

                          TY

Whoa.

                         EDIE

I only stayed friends with you for the gossip.

                       MARSHALL

Don't blame me for your mom leaving ...

                        APRIL

Marshall!

                              TY

Whoa, whoa …


                           MARSHALL

I'm not the one who abandoned you after the accident, so quit using me as a
punching bag for your unresolved guilt! I'm sick of it!


                              EDIE

Get out, you bastard!

        (SHE throws something at him, whatever is close by.)

                           MARSHALL

Gladly!

        (MARSHALL storms off left into his room, slamming the door behind him.)

                             APRIL

What the hell was that, hot wheels?


                              EDIE

Shut up, I don't need your help.


                             APRIL

Of course you do, that's why you keep us around. Oh, and newsflash, Marshall
and I were hooking up all winter.


                              EDIE

I know that. Everybody knows that. Would you just shut up about it?


                              TY

This is not going to end well.

APRIL

Did he talk to you about me?

EDIE

Of course he did, he talks to me about everything. You two would hook up, he'd freak out and run to me. Not any more, though, that's for sure.

APRIL

Why would he talk to you?

EDIE

Everyone thinks the guy is such a genius, but he has no idea what's up and what's down when it comes to relationships!

APRIL

He had no problem knowing what goes up and down with me.

EDIE

Just 'cause a guy will have sex with you doesn't make you likable.

APRIL

At least I don't have to roll all my baggage around with me. No one wants to hook up on the short bus.

TY

Ladies, I think we should take a moment to inhale ...

(MARSHALL storms back into the living room, carrying a suitcase and a backpack.)

MARSHALL

School is done tomorrow. You wanna go nuts and let it all burn? That's on you. I don't have to put up with it.

(HE exits.)

                                        EDIE
Asshole!

        (A long pause.)

                                        TY
Nietzsche said it best when …

                              APRIL and EDIE
Shut up, Ty!

                                        TY
Yes. I will go fold this laundry and leave you to … yes.

        (HE exits. Beat.)

                                        APRIL
So you think I'm a fat slut?

                                        EDIE
You're not fat.

        (Pause.)

I didn't mean that.

                                        APRIL
Slut shaming isn't cool, Edie.

                                        EDIE
I don't know what happened to me.

APRIL

You just totally pissed on your two best friends.

EDIE

I know ...

APRIL

Like stain the carpet, stink up the house, call Stanley Steemer there's piss all over the rug ...

EDIE

I'm sorry, ok?

APRIL

You think sorry's gonna cut it after all that?

EDIE

I don't know what else to say.

APRIL

Are you still hung up on Marshall?

EDIE

I can't deal with this right now.

(SHE wheels herself over to the ramp and tries to set it up again.)

APRIL

Fatty and gimpy are dealing with all kinds of stuff tonight, babe.

(APRIL stands on the board, preventing EDIE from lifting it.)

  EDIE

Move over.

                                        APRIL

No, we're gonna work this out, hot wheels.

                                        EDIE

Don't call me that.

                                        APRIL

You love it when I call you that.

                                        EDIE

No I don't.

                                        APRIL

Yes you do. You've loved it since I called you that freshman year at the ice
cream social.

                                        EDIE

But you were a jerk.

                                        APRIL

You rolled over my foot.

                                        EDIE

Because you were a jerk.

                                        APRIL

Because you rolled over my foot!

        (Pause.)

Can we sit down and talk about this?

EDIE

I'd rather stand if it's alright with you.

(APRIL goes to the couch.)

APRIL

What's going on Edie? I'm supposed to be the loud and emotional one in the loft. I don't like it when you move in on my territory.

EDIE

I'm pregnant, April.

APRIL

You have to get laid before you can get pregnant.

EDIE

Well I'm pregnant.

(A long pause.)

APRIL

Well shit.

(A short pause.)

Who did this? Do you want me to kill him? I'll kill him. I'll gut that son of a bitch like a trout, just say the word. I know a guy who can make it happen, for real, just give me the name, it'll look like an accident. A horrible wood chipper accident.

EDIE

It's not like that. I wanted it. The sex, I mean. I just didn't think ... this would happen.

> APRIL

Why didn't you tell me?

> EDIE

Cause it was nothing.

> APRIL

Cashing in your V-card is not nothing, Edie. You're freaking twenty-two. That's like ninety in virgin years. You should have told me! That's the kind of gossip girls like me live for.

> EDIE

I thought there might be something with the guy, but that's definitely not the case.

> APRIL

Are you gonna keep it? The baby, or nugget, or parasite, whatever, your body your choice.

> EDIE

I don't know.

> APRIL

What about grad school? Holy crap, you can't do this on your own.

> EDIE

Yes, I can.

> APRIL

Edie, this is a baby, not grocery shopping. You can't raise a kid on your own.

> EDIE

My dad did.

APRIL

That's different, and you were like twelve when your mom left. This is not just your life we're talking about anymore. Have you told the father?

EDIE

You can't tell anybody, not until I figure this out, ok?

(EDIE's cell phone beeps. APRIL picks it up.)

Is it Marshall?

APRIL

No, it's Ty. He says "Marshall departed post haste and is unresponsive to my queries. I am in pursuit."

(APRIL begins typing a text message.)

EDIE

What are you doing? Give me my phone!

APRIL

Your fingers are too slow, it's really frustrating.

EDIE

What are you typing?

APRIL

Just telling him to hurry up.

(SHE finishes and tosses the phone on the couch.)

There. What about Marshall?

                              EDIE
What about him?


                              APRIL
Are you going to tell him?


                              EDIE
Tell him what?


                              APRIL
That you're pregnant, doofus.


                              EDIE
He's got enough to worry about.


                              APRIL
He's like your brother, Edie.


                              EDIE
God, he's not my brother! I don't have to tell him anything!


                              APRIL
Fine, chill.


                              EDIE
Sorry.


                              APRIL
So, what about the doctors, what have they said? Is it ok for you to … have a baby?


                              EDIE
I don't know. I've got my first appointment on Tuesday.

APRIL

Is that what … ? I thought it was about your legs or something.

EDIE

I have other doctors besides my neuro-surgeon.

APRIL

I didn't mean …

EDIE

My legs may not work but my hoo-ha is just fine.

APRIL

So it seems. Can I go with? You could use the support, and I love getting the good parking spots.

EDIE

You think I should keep it?

APRIL

I think you should to shave your legs if you're going to the hoo-ha doctor.

EDIE

Shaving my legs is what got me into this mess.

APRIL

Gynos judge you if you haven't shaved, you know that right? Come on, let's get you looking less like a sasquatch while I paint my toenails. I'll do yours, if you want.

(APRIL sets the ramp back up.)

EDIE

Yes, please. My doc's a guy, Dr. Robert. I've got to look nice.

APRIL

Oh, then we've got a lot of work to do. Get in there.

EDIE

Hey. It's "Get in there, hot wheels," to you.

APRIL

Yes, ma'am. I'm right behind you.

> (EDIE is off. APRIL picks up EDIE's cell phone from the couch. APRIL searches, mumbling to herself.)

Marshall, Marshall …

> (SHE finds his number.)

Here we go …

> (SHE types him a text message and then sends it. SHE puts the phone back down on the couch and then heads for the bathroom.)

And send. Coming!

> (SHE is off. A moment later, TY enters singing carrying folded laundry.)

TY

"My body's saying let's go, but my heart is saying no."

> (HE looks around.)

> TY (con't)

Hello? Anybody here? Silence is a true friend who never betrays.

(EDIE's cell phone beeps. HE looks around and then reads the message.)

And so it begins.

## END OF PLAY

# Of or Like "the Real": An Exercise on Realism

1. Re-read "Revolver" with tenets of Realism in mind. In this case, note that the play has identifiable characters, and the manner in which they speak is contemporaneous for the time period.
2. Consider, what, specifically, in terms of action, setting, and props, makes this realistic (of or like "the real"). List those.
3. List all aspects of set pieces, props (both hand held objects and set dressing) that contribute to making the atmosphere similar to everyday life.
4. Share your list.

# For Further Research

Bailey, Sally. *Barrier-Free Theatre: Including Everyone in Theatre Arts—in Schools, Recreation, and Arts Programs—Regardless of (Dis)Ability.* Enumclaw, WA: Idyll Arbor, 2010.

Fahy, Tom, and Kimball, King, eds. *Peering Behind the Curtain: Disability, Illness, and the Extraordinary Body in Contemporary Theatre.* New York: Routledge, 2012.

Kempe, Andy. *Drama, Disability and Education: A Critical Exploration for Students and Practitioners.* New York: Routledge, 2012.

(Also see the "For Further Research" section for Bianca Sams's play "Supernova.")

CHAPTER 11

# Scott R. Irelan

PLAYWRIGHT

## *FIREWORKS*
©2015 Scott R. Irelan

**PRODUCTION HISTORY**

"Fireworks" was first seen as part of the Chicago Dramatists' Saturday Series in 2004. Since then, it has undergone a major revision and is awaiting production.

CAST OF CHARACTERS
    ESPERANZA
    TONY

    SETTING—The newest, nicest place on the banks of the Detroit River. It is July 4, 2004.

# About the Playwright

Scott R. Irelan is Associate Dean of Fine Arts at Western Michigan University, where he is also a tenured faculty member in the Department of Theatre. He previously served as chairperson of Theatre and Dance at Youngstown State University, where he was a tenured member of the Department of Theatre and Dance. Irelan has also held positions at Augustana College (in Illinois) and Illinois State University. He earned his PhD from Southern Illinois University, and both his MA and BA from Bowling Green State University. Irelan is primarily a theatre historian and dramaturg. Other areas of interest to him are new play development, directing, and nontraditional scripting.

Some of Irelan's professional dramaturgy work has taken him to the Riverside Theatre Shakespeare Festival in Iowa City, Iowa; the Illinois Shakespeare Festival in Normal, Illinois; and the Boston Playwrights' Theatre. Irelan is past coordinator of dramaturgy and past vice-chair of New Plays for the Kennedy Center American College Theatre Festival, Region III. In these capacities, he introduced "Design Storm" (a collaborative activity based on exercises he and Anne Fletcher developed at SIU), new play dramaturgy to the 10-minute play portion of the regional festival, and a regional production note award for dramaturgs. His academic writings have appeared in *Journal of American Drama and Theatre, Theatre Journal, Modernism/Modernity, Theatre History Studies,* and *Shakespeare Bulletin,* among others. The coauthored *The Process of Dramaturgy* is available from Focus Publishing, *Experiencing Theatre* (with Anne Fletcher) is obtainable from Hackett Publishing, and his *Enacting Nationhood* is available from Cambridge Scholars Publishing. Irelan's latest full-length play, *Lake Affect,* is currently under review by several theatres.

# Form and Style

Irelan's dramatic writing, whether full-length or short-form, sometimes uses the conventions of playwriting to lead readers and watchers alike to what the motion picture industry often refers to as a **perception shift**. Regardless of content, Irelan works to craft a dramatic story that engages the audience and then seemingly pulls their attention in a different direction at the last possible moment. Upon further review, it becomes clear that Irelan has embedded small clues along the way, the sum of which explains the perception shift (usually by the play's end). "Fireworks" is a good example of this.

Esperanza, a dancer at Eisenhower Contemporary Dance Company who aged out of foster care not too long ago, has been dreaming of connecting with Tony on a deeper level. When she arrives at the condo after a long day of rehearsals for her soon-to-be-here opening night, Tony is sitting at the table reworking a report that someone else needed to do. He is a well-known area businessman who likes to invest more in work than in anything (or anyone) else. Though they have a formalized *seekingarrangement.com* agreement, Tony's work habits are the root of Esperanza's problems. A seemingly benign look at the day's mail escalates. After Esperanza pushes Tony to the brink of opening up to her, which he honestly considers doing, Tony returns to his priority—work. Devastated, Esperanza decides to break the arrangement and leave him. Tony works his charm offensive on her. Just as the fireworks outside begin, Esperanza makes sure that he knows where she stands on this issue: she is done with him. The microaggressions day after day have grown to be too much for her.

Reread the summary in the preceding paragraph. Pause for a moment. Consider how the script is being described to you. Now decide whether or not this might be Realism or non-Realism as we discussed in the introduction. So, what did you pick? If you deduced that "Fireworks" probably takes both the form and style of Theatrical Realism, then you are right. What clues in the description did you use to arrive at this decision? Was it the indication of an actual dance company? Was it character names and occupations that sound like those from our daily, lived experiences? Now, before reading the actual script, do a little dramaturgical research into the setting of the play and the dance company that Esperanza works for at the time we meet her. What does that tell you about her? As you turn to reading the full text of the play, pay close attention to how the conversations between Esperanza and Tony go back and forth like those you might have. Lastly, see if you can figure out what the perception shift might be, *before* you get to the last page of the play. Were you right? What clue or clues did you find most helpful in figuring it out? Was there an element of surprise to it? Why or why not?

# Plays for Further Study

Some model plays for further study would be *The Nerd* by Larry Shue, *The Mousetrap* by Agatha Christie, *Valparaiso* by Don DeLillo, and *Tranced* by Bob Clyman. Shue introduces us to architect Willum Cubbert and fellow ex-GI Rick Steadman, whom Cubbert has never seen but who did save Cubbert's life in Vietnam. The bumbling Rick arrives on Willum's birthday, and antics, including a twist ending, ensue. A classic mystery in content, *The Mousetrap* takes us on a journey with snow-trapped travelers, one of whom is a murderer. At its core, *Valparaiso* is about the power of media and its intense influence on the lives of individuals; the ending of DeLillo's 1999 play will certainly involve you in a perception shift. *Tranced* by Bob Clyman dives into the dependability of remembrances, the power of suggestion, and what happens when the two collide. When examining these plays, take note of how each writer uses the form to carry us through a story that has a shift in perception some-where late in the play.

The next four plays all have two main characters and intense situations, not unlike what "Fireworks" offers. While there is a sense of perception-shifting in these, what is more interesting to look at is the way the writers have developed the dialogue between characters. *True West* by Sam Shepard is sometimes fondly referred to as the "toaster play," for a key scene in Act Two. Austin and Lee are brothers. One is a petty thief, the other a writer penning a screenplay. Eventually they switch roles. In *Oleanna*, David Mamet examines the struggles of university professor John and his student Carol, who has accused him of sexual exploitation, which ruins his chances for tenure. In the Pulitzer Prize–winning *Topdog/Underdog*, by Suzan-Lori Parks, the two characters we follow are brothers Lincoln and Booth. Sarah Ruhl's *Dear Elizabeth* reveals the friendship between poets Elizabeth Bishop and Robert Lowell through the dramatic sharing of some of the eight hundred pages of letters they wrote to one another over the years. As you read through these, pay special attention to the way your body feels as the writers skillfully escalate the incidents.

## CAUTION

Professionals and amateurs are hereby notified that all plays are under copyright and permission must be obtained to use them in any manner. All rights, including professional and amateur stage rights, motion picture, recitation, lecturing, public reading, radio broadcasting, television, video or sound recording, all other forms of mechanical or electronic reproduction, and the rights of translation into foreign languages, are strictly reserved. All inquiries concerning rights, including amateur rights, should be addressed to the writer or writer's agent.

# FIREWORKS

CAST OF CHARACTERS
   ESPERANZA—Twenty-one, proficient dancer at Eisenhower Dance
   TONY—Older than Esperanza, well known in business

   SETTING—The newest, nicest place on the banks of the Detroit River. It is
July 4, 2004.

**AT RISE:** It has rained. The humidity is on the rise. TONY sits at the table reading a report. ESPERANZA enters in rehearsal clothes. SHE keeps her hands in the pocket of her hoodie as much as possible. Soft strains of No Doubt's "It's My Life" fade out as the lights come up. This is what ESPERANZA is listening to as SHE enters. This is a tense place full of microaggressions that grow.

ESPERANZA

Hey.

TONY

Hi.

ESPERANZA

Good day?

(Kisses TONY on the cheek. ESPERANZA goes immediately to the kitchen.)

TONY

Not great.

                         ESPERANZA
Yeah.

                           TONY
Had to go to the gym and work it off.

                         ESPERANZA
        (Rooting through the fridge)
You hate those crowds.

        (Beat.)

Where's the dip?

                           TONY
In front of the fridge.

                         ESPERANZA
Ha. Ha.

                           TONY
Third shelf. In the back.

                         ESPERANZA
Got it.

                           TONY
Thought I should hide it so you wouldn't eat too much. Big opening soon and all.

                         ESPERANZA
Always looking out for me. That's why I love this.

        (Closes fridge. ESPERANZA takes dip and bottled water to the counter
        looks for the chips.)

TONY

Hmm. And I thought it was my devilish charm.

(There is a whole ritual of noise as ESPERANZA opens the chips, finds the perfect one, dips it, chomps, and repeats. Each sound visibly aggravates TONY.)

I have got to have this expense report revised by tomorrow. Idiots in procurement …

ESPERANZA

Ah. If anyone can do it, you can. Just remember that we all can't be as brilliant as you.

(TONY rolls eyes and returns to the report.)

What do you think of my see-food diet?

TONY

Another diet!

ESPERANZA

See. Food.

TONY

Sometimes you act like you're—

ESPERANZA

Do you really want to talk about age my dear?

TONY

No. Just maturity levels.

(ESPERANZA gingerly looks for quieter snack food. No luck.)

> ESPERANZA

Oh. Almost forgot. Here's the mail.

> TONY

Great.

> ESPERANZA

Mostly bills.

    (Beat.)

The country club.

> TONY

Oh boy.

> ESPERANZA

Your cell.

> TONY

Uh huh.

> ESPERANZA

And last. But certainly not least. Drum roll please.

    (Beat.)

Drum roll please.

    (TONY does so with little enthusiasm.)

A wedding invitation.

                                TONY
Hunh.

                              ESPERANZA
That got me thinking about the Keys.

                                TONY
Yes.

                              ESPERANZA
God. What a night. Bobby. Mary Jane. And gin martinis.

                                TONY
Too many gin martinis.

                              ESPERANZA
Had to spend all night nursing you back to health.

                                TONY
And *that's* why I need you.

        (TONY crosses to ESPERANZA. THEY kiss. TONY fixes a drink. ESPERANZA
        sneaks over to table to look at the invitation TONY has left out and open.)

                              ESPERANZA
So.

                                TONY
        (Fixing a sandwich)
Get away from that.

ESPERANZA

The invitation.

TONY

Yes.

ESPERANZA

Come on.

TONY

My sister.

ESPERANZA

Little Ameya's getting married!

TONY

Can't pick your in-laws.

ESPERANZA

That's for sure.

TONY

Guy is a real piece of/work.

ESPERANZA

Designer or off the rack?

TONY

Now he thinks he wants to be an auto mechanic. Nothing wrong with that. I mean those guys on NPR do it. They have PhDs from MIT though. She has this whole working-class thing going on right now. I was hoping she would work out of it.

ESPERANZA

Designer or off the rack?

(Silence.)

TONY

I told you when we started this that personal prying was off limits.

ESPERANZA

That was three years ago. I love Ameya.

TONY

Sure Ameya would be fine with it. But my parents would. This is not part/
of the …

ESPERANZA

Are you kidding me with this?

TONY

I told you—

ESPERANZA

I know. I know. I just thought—

TONY

You thought wrong.

ESPERANZA

Always do.

TONY

This … arrangement is just not something you talk about …

ESPERANZA

Ever!

TONY

That's the beauty of it. I don't have to. You signed. I sealed it. That's it.

ESPERANZA

Sometimes I just lay under you and think about how much I want to cry.

TONY

This is not up for discussion. I—

ESPERANZA

Yes m'lord.

TONY

    (Gets slightly physical)
Knock it off.

ESPERANZA

    (Returning the favor)
No. No. You knock it off.

TONY

What are you ...

    (Beat.)

ESPERANZA

I'm tired of this. This. Whatever this is.

TONY

So am I.

ESPERANZA

Then stop closing /

TONY

Never get personal. Rule number/one.

ESPERANZA

Stop closing off whenever it comes up. She knows.

TONY

Of course. She knew before I told her.

ESPERANZA

It's just the rest of them.

TONY

What happens behind these …

ESPERANZA

Yes. Tony. Yes.

TONY

I've got to get back to work.

ESPERANZA

Here we go with this again.

TONY

I'm the one supporting your dance "career."

ESPERANZA

I earned that spot.

                    TONY

And I sustain you in it.

                  ESPERANZA

I've got my own money.

                    TONY

From the allowance.

                  ESPERANZA

No you jerk. From dancing with Eisenhower.

     (TONY returns fully to the report. ESPERANZA has been closed out.)

Sonofabitch. You'd find an excuse to revise your grocery list just so you wouldn't
have to deal with this. With me.

                    TONY

What?

                  ESPERANZA

Don't play dumb. DO NOT play dumb. It doesn't become you. You do this every
time I—

                    TONY

—talk about THIS? What? What is THIS?

                  ESPERANZA

Your feelings. Your emotions. Us. Tony. Us.

                    TONY

I have ...

ESPERANZA

... have certain expectations of privacy.


TONY

Yes.


ESPERANZA

(Starts jamming items into her bag)

Believe me. I know all about your expectations. You have no idea what I've given up for you. I swallowed my pride. I signed your agreement.


TONY

Everyone makes sacrifices.


ESPERANZA

Not you. You sit there with your expectations. And your work. And your buffer zone.


TONY

Our family name carries with it a certain ...


ESPERANZA

Are you kidding me with this right now?


TONY

You know I don't kid.


ESPERANZA

Really? You. No. I'd never guess.


TONY

It's easy for you. Family's not an issue.

ESPERANZA

Right. Aging out of foster care is a real badge of honor.

(TONY looks ready to engage, physically or otherwise, but does not.)

Here we go. Brick by brick.

TONY

That's right. Up goes the fucking wall.

(TONY throws his drink against the wall. HE returns to the report staring forward. ESPERANZA is behind him doing the same. The fireworks outside begin to accelerate.)

ESPERANZA

This used to be fun.

TONY

I know.

(Beat.)

I need you.

ESPERANZA

That's what you tell me.

(Beat.)

TONY

It's just hard for me.

ESPERANZA

I know.

(TONY crosses to ESPERANZA. HE embraces ESPERANZA from behind. ESPERANZA pulls away and heads toward the door, hand on the handle.)

TONY

There's nothing better for you out there.

ESPERANZA

(Turning around)

Tell Ameya she's beautiful for me.

(TONY has his hand out. ESPERANZA takes it, slowly. SHE knew HE would make this kind of move. In grand Judas-style, ESPERANZA kisses TONY. As ESPERANZA does, we hear a gunshot at the same time as the fireworks outside. TONY stares into ESPERANZA's eyes. ESPERANZA lays TONY on the floor, careful to get no blood on the workout clothing. All we see is TONY's face with blank stare peeking out from behind the counter, as the life runs out of him. Jacques Lu Cont's Thin White Duke Remix of "It's My Life" comes in as we watch for a moment. SHE grabs the invitation and some money, stepping over his body. ESPERANZA calls the police from her Nokia. SHE reports a shooting in self-defense. The rest of the conversation trails off as SHE exits. Lights slowly fade out. The last thing we see is TONY's face, staring.)

## END OF PLAY

# What Just Happened?: An Exercise on Perception Shifting

1. Locate a print magazine and have at the ready a favorite tweet or other social media post of 140 or less characters.
2. Randomly open the magazine and point. The nearest image is the setting for your two-character scene.
3. The tweet or social media post is the first line. For the purposes of this exercise just use A and B to indicate character names.
4. Set an alarm for two minutes and start it as soon as you have written the first line. Free-write the dialogue.
5. When the alarm goes off, turn to another page of the magazine, close your eyes, point. The nearest sentence is your next line. Start the two minute timer. Continue to write.
6. When the alarm sounds, choose a favorite fairy tale or animated character (i.e., Winnie the Pooh). Use their given name. This character now enters the play as one of the other characters exits. Set the timer and write.
7. Once the alarm sounds, spend the last two minutes of the exercise by ending the play with the characters you have created enacting a historic event (i.e., the ratification of the 19th Amendment).
8. Read out loud, preferably to someone else. Take note of the drastic shifts and unexpected turns. When revising, think about what bridge dialogue, stage direction, or other creative interventions might be needed if you were to continue to turn this into a ten minute play.

## For Further Research

Dunne, Will. *The Dramatic Writer's Companion: Tools to Develop Characters, Cause Scenes, and Build Stories.* Chicago: University of Chicago Press, 2009.

Friedmann, Anthony. *Writing for Visual Media.* 4th ed. New York and London: Focal Press, 2014.

Mamet, David. *Three Uses of the Knife: On the Nature and Purpose of Drama.* New York: Vintage Books, 1998.

Ruhl, Sarah. *100 Essays I Don't Have Time to Write: On Umbrellas and Sword Fights, Parades and Dogs, Fire Alarms, Children, and Theater.* New York: Farrar, Straus and Giroux, 2014.

Wright, Michael. *Sensory Writing for Stage and Screen: An Etude-Based Process of Exploration.* Cambridge, MA: Hackett Publishing, 2015.

# CHAPTER 12

# Kirsten Easton

PLAYWRIGHT

## *THE BATHING SUITS*

©2015 Kirsten Easton

### PRODUCTION HISTORY

"The Bathing Suits" is one play within Kirsten Easton's curated work *Girls with Bodies*, which was first performed at Southern Illinois University's Big Muddy Play Festival, March–April 2015.

CAST OF CHARACTERS
    GIRL 1
    GIRL 2
    GIRL 3
    GIRL 4
    GIRL 5
    GIRL 6

SETTING—A department store fitting room. Present.

# *FIT*

## PRODUCTION HISTORY

"Fit" was first performed at the Kennedy Center American College Theatre Festival in Milwaukee, Wisconsin, in January 2014.

## CAST OF CHARACTERS
POLLY
BETTY

SETTING—A department store dressing room. Present.

## About the Playwright

Kirsten Easton is a Southern California native who recently completed an MFA in Playwriting at Southern Illinois University. She is particularly interested in exploring gender and sexuality by using the conventions of theatre to shed new light on these topics. Given this, she focuses on subjects that are typically off-limits, with most of what we might consider "private conversations" being fair game in her plays. This approach allows Easton to intertwine her feminist values with humor and candor, affording her the opportunity to make a larger point without being heavy-handed. Prior to attending graduate school, Easton worked for Native Voices at the Autry Museum of the American West and received her BA from Occidental College in both Theatre and Sociology. Her interest in sociology manifests in the subject matter of much of her work. Most recently, this came through in her full-length play *Wife/Worker/Whore*, inspired by Norma Jean Almodovar's *From Cop to Call Girl*, a book that Easton read for a sociology class entitled Power and Sexuality. *Wife/Worker/Whore* questions whether or not the institution of marriage is really a sanctioned form of prostitution, asking if a woman's sleeping with her husband or boss for money is the same as sex for hire. In a similar vein, *Trixxxie 2.0* offers possession of a sex-robot as an alternative to a real, in-the-flesh relationship with a human being in order to question the nature of relationships, intimacy, and the unrealistic expectations that are often imposed on women by their male partners.

Many readers and watchers alike have found Easton's dialogue accessible and the subject matter of her plays relevant to their lived experience. In her artistic statement, the playwright states, "My plays take you to the places that you never thought you'd go and sometimes never wanted to either."

Easton has recently taught classes in introduction to the theatre and play analysis. In addition to teaching, she has served as Coordinator of Graduate Teaching Support at the Center for Teaching Excellence. She has presented in the Pedagogy Symposium at the Mid-America Theatre Conference (MATC), where her plays have been read and produced as well. Recent staged readings of other Easton works include *The Lovers* at MadLab Theatre in Columbus, Ohio, and *Adrift* at Spring Cleaning Festival at the Arkansas Theatre Collective. Still other original works have been read and performed in Los Angeles, Chicago, and Carbondale, Illinois. Find and follow Kirsten Easton on twitter (@easton_kirsten), or visit her website http://kirsteneaston.wix.com/playwright.

## Form and Style

Many of Easton's works, both short and full-length, explore ways in which women often feel expected to put on a perfect veneer, sweeping their hopes, dreams, embarrassments, and shame under the rug. Body image and self-esteem are themes with which her plays (and characters) grapple, and her pieces often offer young women options they might not have previously considered. At other times, the plays put on display real-life concerns with which audiences and readers can identify.

Both "The Bathing Suits" and "Fit" use shopping and selection of clothing to address both the theme of body image and the feelings of inadequacy and humiliation that often confront women as a result of their imperfect bodies. In "Fit" we see a mother/daughter relationship, and the judgmental manner in which well-meaning mothers sometimes speak to their offspring about self, body, diet, and physical well-being. "The Bathing Suits" features anthropomorphized garments, begging to be selected by the shopper. "Fit" is cast in the form of Realism, with contemporary, believable dialogue, conversation drawn from every day life, and a common, recognizable setting. "The Bathing Suits," on the other hand, approaches the story it tells from a different place. Although the play's language is both recognizable and clear, and the setting is a dressing room such as we might find at any mall, this play moves out of the realm of Realism and into that of the hybrid play largely for two reasons. First, the character names represent the function of each within the plot. Second, the garments are anthropomorphized. In fact, we might go as far as to suggest that elements of the play as written are borrowed from Expressionism (that is, epithets instead of character names and rapid-fire dialogue in staccato bursts). A production team could explore distorting the fitting room mirrors, and, possibly, instead of witnessing an onstage transformation of shoppers becoming suits, a single shopper could be dwarfed in the presence of the competing demands of one bathing suit over another one. Mark Fortier provides a good starting point for thinking about feminist critical theory, which is another way to look at the following plays:

> Feminist theory is profoundly concerned with the cultural representation of women, sometimes strictly masculinist fantasy with no relation to real women, sometimes as the appropriation of women and women's bodies to masculine perspectives. ... The body is one site of oppression for women; subjectivity is another (*Theatre/Theory: An Introduction* (2nd ed.) [New York: Routledge, 2002] 111).

In our experience, and as suggested by Fortier, feminist critical theory provides a way of seeing certain ideologies that have limited the subjectivity of women in daily, material life. It is also important to make note of the polyvocality of both of these short plays. This writing style is often a hallmark of feminist writing. In this case, **polyvocality** can be found in the overlapping dialogue, characters interrupting each other, and the ways that this constitutes the multiple "voices" of mother, sister, boyfriend, and sales clerk, reverberating in the shopper's mind, with all their attendant baggage. By looking at "The Bathing Suits" and "Fit" through this particular lens, we should begin to see ways in which women are sometimes "objectified" in contemporary culture. Following that line of reasoning, we can begin to recognize how films, television shows, novels, other plays, and even real-life situations are illustrated from the perspective that Jill Dolan, Laura Mulvey, and other feminist critics and scholars have dubbed "the male gaze"—a system of culture-based representation that silences and distorts the lived realities of females. Kirsten Easton works to combat this perspective in her works.

# Plays for Further Study

The playwright herself has cited George Bernard Shaw's *Mrs. Warren's Profession* as thematic inspiration for her work. Henrik Ibsen's *A Doll's House,* with Torvald's diminutive language in reference to his wife, comes to mind as another appropriate play to study. Other possible choices are Ntozake Shange's choreopoem *For Colored Girls Who Have Considered Suicide/When the Rainbow Is Enuf* for its style, or Sophie Treadwell's expressionistic *Machinal* with its staccato and overlapping dialogue. There are several plays by a range of contemporary female playwrights that might be paired with Easton's short play for further study as they relate to body image, body awareness, and "popularity" as social constructs of oppression. *The Waiting Room* by Lisa Loomer, *Body Awareness* by Annie Baker, and *Real Girls Can't Win* by Merri Biechler immediately come to mind.

## CAUTION

# THE BATHING SUITS

CAST OF CHARACTERS
    GIRL 1
    GIRL 2
    GIRL 3
    GIRL 4
    GIRL 5
    GIRL 6

    SETTING—A department store fitting room. Present.

> **AT RISE:** We are in a Department Store Fitting Room. The selection process has started. The Bathing Suits are in competition for attention.

GIRL 4

Which bathing suit are you going to buy?

GIRL 2

Which one?

GIRL 5

Which suit?

GIRL 3

You can only pick one.

GIRL 6

Just one?

GIRL 1

You can only have one suit.

GIRL 3

I'm the sexy halter bikini. I tie in the back of your neck and around your back. I come with matching sexy bottoms. Dazzle at the beach in this spicy combo.

GIRL 1

I'm the modest, yet sexy Tankini. I provide more tummy coverage. Unlike the sexy halter bikini. If you're looking for beauty and simplicity, look no further than this tankini.

GIRL 3

Coverage is not sexy.

GIRL 2

I'm the super skimpy string bikini. Strings hold me together. Strings on your neck. String on your back and strings on your hips. Grab everyone's attention in this tiny suit.

GIRL 5

Strings hold together and strings fall apart.

GIRL 6

There aren't any one-pieces?

GIRL 2

No one-pieces. Those don't exist.

GIRL 6

Are you sure?

GIRL 3

Only two.

GIRL 1

Modest.

GIRL 3

Dazzle.

GIRL 5

I'm the closest you can get to a one-piece. Behold the monokini. Mono meaning one and kini meaning lots of cut outs! I cover all the important parts, but show off all the others! If you're looking for a more sophisticated take on the average bathing suit, look no further than right here. The monokini.

GIRL 6

You sure do show a lot of skin.

GIRL 4

Do you get tired of straps digging into your neck? Do you think straps or strings are unsightly or annoying? Well look no more! I am here! This season's sexy bandeau top! I'm basically just a ring of fabric that covers your breasts. But oh, do I cover them well!

GIRL 2

Skimpy!

GIRL 5

Cut-outs!

GIRL 1

Which suit will you choose?

GIRL 4

So many choices.

GIRL 5

Mono means one!

GIRL 3

Try me on!

GIRL 1

No, try me on!

GIRL 2

I'm the best suit!

GIRL 5

I'm the most flattering.

GIRL 4

Choose me, you won't be sorry.

(GIRL 6 chooses the string bikini. GIRL 2 mirrors GIRL 6's movements, as if GIRL 6 is trying on the string bikini. All of the Bathing Suits make an oohing noise of disapproval.)

GIRL 1

That is not the right suit for you.

GIRL 5

Very unflattering.

GIRL 4

You need fewer strings.

GIRL 3

I don't know what it is.

GIRL 2

Take me off!

(GIRL 2 exits.)

GIRL 5

Here, try me on.

(GIRL 6 tries on the monokini. GIRL 5 mirrors her movements just as GIRL 2 did. The Bathing Suits again make an oohing noise of disapproval.)

GIRL 4

Nope. Nope. Nope.

GIRL 1

Not for you.

GIRL 3

*I* come in six different colors.

GIRL 5

Take me off!

(GIRL 5 exits.)

GIRL 3

You know, I think it's time to take me for a spin.

(GIRL 6 tries halter bikini. GIRL 3 mirrors her, just as the others before. The Bathing Suits laugh.)

GIRL 1

I'm sorry. I'm sorry, I shouldn't be laughing.

GIRL 4

She looks hysterical!

                    GIRL 1
Hilarious!

                    GIRL 3
Take me off.

     (GIRL 3 exits.)

                    GIRL 4
There's only two of us left.

                    GIRL 1
Perhaps a tankini would be more flattering.

                    GIRL 4
If halter bikini didn't work, you know I'm here for you.

                    GIRL 1
Try me on!

                    GIRL 4
No—try me on!

                    GIRL 6
I don't like either of you.

                    GIRL 1
What will you wear to the beach?

                    GIRL 4
Or the pool?

                    GIRL 1
You aren't going to go naked are you?

                                    GIRL 6

You sound like my mother.


                                    GIRL 1

I am your mother.


                                    GIRL 4

I'm the voice of your mother too!


                                    GIRL 1

And your sister.


                                    GIRL 4

And your first boyfriend.


                                    GIRL 1

And that moody salesclerk at the department store.


                                    GIRL 6

Enough! I just won't go swimming anymore. I won't have to worry about it.


                                    GIRL 4

No more swimming?


                                    GIRL 1

No more?


                                    GIRL 6

Not with these choices.


**END OF PLAY**

# FIT

CAST OF CHARACTERS
     POLLY—An 11-year-old girl
     BETTY—Her mother

     SETTING—A Department Store Dressing Room. Present.

**AT RISE:** A dressing room stall. BETTY stands just outside of the stall, waiting for her daughter, POLLY.

BETTY

Polly, I don't have all day.

POLLY (off)

I'll be out in a second, ma.

BETTY

How long does it take to try on clothes?

POLLY (off)

I have a hard time getting stuff off.

BETTY

You have a hard time not staring at yourself in the mirror.

POLLY (off)

I'm not looking at myself in the mirror.

BETTY

Get out here and show me.

(POLLY peeks her head out.)

                          POLLY
I don't think you want to see this.

                          BETTY
Why not?

                          POLLY
It doesn't look very good.

                          BETTY
What do you mean it doesn't look good?

                          POLLY
It's not worth showing you.

                          BETTY
Get out here.

        (POLLY slowly exits the dressing room stall.)

                          POLLY
Well.

                          BETTY
Why aren't your pants buttoned?

                          POLLY
They're not? I must have forgotten.

                          BETTY
Well button them then.

                                   POLLY
They're comfortable this way. I don't need to.

                                   BETTY
You may as well not even wear pants if you are going to walk around with them
unbuttoned.

                                   POLLY
You mean walk around in my underwear?

                                   BETTY
Don't be cute. Now, do them up.

                                   POLLY
Fine.

     (POLLY makes a few attempts to button her pants, sucking it in and moving
     around, even bracing herself up against the wall, but no luck. The pants
     remain unbuttoned.)

I can't get them.

                                   BETTY
You aren't trying hard enough.

     (BETTY grabs the two sides of POLLY's jeans and tries to make them meet.
     SHE, too, has no luck.)

Well, you must be wearing the wrong size. I'll go get you another pair.

                                   POLLY
They're a Seven.

                    BETTY
A Seven?! You can't fit into a Seven?


                    POLLY
I just can't get them buttoned.


                    BETTY
Didn't I buy you new jeans last Christmas? What size were they?


                    POLLY
Seven.


                    BETTY
And what's wrong with those?


                    POLLY
They're just—they're kind of tight.


                    BETTY
How can that be?


                    POLLY
I don't know. I grew?


                    BETTY
I can't believe that you wasted my money on those jeans.


                    POLLY
It's not like I did it on purpose.


                    BETTY
Someone has been eating too many sweets. I told you at Thanksgiving. Only one slice of chocolate pie per day. But no— you had to eat the whole damn thing!

POLLY

I was hungry.

BETTY

You need to think about eating healthy things when you are hungry. Not gorging yourself on pie.

POLLY

But ma—

BETTY

There's simply no other explanation. Little girls who don't eat pie don't grow that quickly.

POLLY

I think I grew half an inch taller since the last time I measured.

BETTY

Take them off.

POLLY

What? Why?

BETTY

There's no point in standing in the middle of the store with your pants unbuttoned. Put your clothes back on. We're leaving.

POLLY

I'm sorry about the pie.

BETTY

It's not like you can take it back. You can't un-eat it.

POLLY

But I don't have anything else to wear.


BETTY

You have a closet full of clothes. Or did I buy all of those things for another, more grateful girl?


POLLY

They don't fit anymore.


BETTY

How is that possible? How do none of your clothes from last year fit? What about that dress that grandma bought you?


POLLY

That dress is ugly.


BETTY

It is not. It's very becoming.


POLLY

It looks like a dress that Grandma would wear.


BETTY

Your grandmother gets compliments on her appearance all of the time.


POLLY

I don't want to look like Grandma.


BETTY

You should be so lucky. You unfortunately look like your father's side.

POLLY

Please, ma. I think I can make the jeans fit. Just let me try to stretch them out.

(POLLY does some lunges around the room, trying to stretch the jeans out.)

BETTY

I don't have time for this. Take the pants off and get dressed.

POLLY

But I was going to wear jeans on the first day of school.

BETTY

Who says that you're even getting new clothes now?

POLLY

How come?

BETTY

You think little girls who can't fit into a size Seven deserve to get new clothes?

POLLY

I'm not trying to be difficult, I just—

BETTY

Well, you certainly are succeeding, aren't you?

(A silence.)

Paulina. You are a beautiful girl. But you are ruining what God gave you by eating all of those sweets.

POLLY

What are you talking about?

BETTY

What I'm saying is, maybe you should focus on eating healthier and exercising and by Christmas, we can come back and buy you new size Seven jeans. How does that sound?

(A silence. POLLY disappears into the dressing room stall. SHE re-enters.)

POLLY

Can we go now? I don't want to shop anymore.

BETTY

Yes dear. How about we get you a salad for dinner?

POLLY

Um—

(Sighs.)

Ok, ma. Ok.

## END OF PLAY

# Group Playwriting: An Exercise on Feminist Theory

Form groups of 3–5. These should be randomly assigned.

1. List words that relate to body image. Work at separate locations, using butcher-block paper or a whiteboard or chalkboard to make an inventory of words.
2. Select a setting/situation in which most of the words might work (for example, a dressing room).
3. Choose at least two but no more than six characters who might use the vocabulary. Let the vocabulary help you decide on the characters' relationships to each other.
4. Use the words to improvise sentences or lines of dialogue. Get on your feet. Have a note-taker record what is said. Rotate who takes notes and who improvises.
5. Try to establish enough improvised lines to write a five-page text.
6. Read what you have, and work to build a script with a message regarding "body image."

# For Further Research

Aston, Elaine. *An Introduction to Feminism and Theatre.* New York: Routledge, 1995.

Austin, Gayle. *Feminist Theories for Dramatic Criticism.* Ann Arbor, MI: University of Michigan Press, 1991.

Dolan, Jill. *The Feminist Spectator as Critic.* 2nd ed. Ann Arbor, MI: University of Michigan Press, 2012.

——*The Feminist Spectator in Action: Feminist Criticism for the Stage and Screen.* New York: Palgrave Macmillan, 2013.

Fortier, Mark. *Theory/Theatre: An Introduction.* 2nd ed. New York: Routledge, 2002.

# CHAPTER 13

# Jacob Juntunen

## PLAYWRIGHT

## *THE FIRST YES*
©2014 Jacob Juntunen

**PRODUCTION HISTORY**

"The First Yes" was first produced as part of Southern Illinois University's Big Muddy Shorts, a monthly festival for the performance of original short plays.

CAST OF CHARACTERS
    ERIN
    RUSS

    SETTING—An empty stage

# About the Playwright

Originally from California, with a BA from Reed College and advanced degrees from Ohio University (MA) and Northwestern University (PhD), Jacob Juntunen heads the Playwriting programs at Southern Illinois University. He has extensive experience in the Chicago storefront theatre scene, as an alumnus Senior Network Playwright at Chicago Dramatists, as the founding managing director of Mortar Theatre, and as a recipient of a Community Arts Assistance Program (CAAP) grant. He is also the author of "Black and White", which appears in this collection.

# Form and Style

In this short play, a married couple, both English professors and poets, confront the present circumstances of their life (Russ's mortality) and play out their memories of the last evening of Russ's life, in their backyard, surrounded by friends, on the occasion of publication of the husband's last book of poetry. They speak of their "legacies": their books and, more importantly, their daughter Ava, now a senior in college. The play's title, "The First Yes," refers to the moment when Erin knew that she would spend her life married to Russ; and in the play, as she faces his terminal cancer, she wonders about the other path she might have taken, without Russ, had she not said "yes" to him. Time is mutable in this play; past juxtaposes present. Dialogue flows smoothly between the two as the characters move swiftly from one to the other, as with Russ's lines "What *was* I going to tell Ava? "What *am* I going to tell Ava?." Erin opens the play as narrator, and throughout the play she and Russ speak not only to each other, but also to us, the reader/audience as well, commenting on their feelings. In this way, Juntunen creates a hybrid piece, rooted in everyday life but tinged with the **theatrical convention** (a rule about the world of the play) of spoken memory and of commentary that is out of sync with the forward action of the play but not jarring. Juntunen interjects wry humor into what could become a morbid play through the couple's spats, the coupling of mosquitoes with the beauty of the starlit backyard, and his clever, intellectual jibes at twenty-first-century academics and their self-consciousness. Interwoven within the arc of the play are not really subplots, but rather parallel stories—of the loss of the family's dogs, of the couple's experience as "empty nesters"—that are part and parcel of the lived experience of living, loving, and letting go.

# Plays for Further Study

Characters die in many plays, but two in particular pair nicely with "The First Yes": Thornton Wilder's 1938 classic, *Our Town*, and Margaret Edson's Pulitzer Prize-winning *Wit* (1999). In *Our Town*, Wilder traces the life of a married couple, George and Emily, through childhood and adolescence and marriage, to the time of Emily's death and George's inconsolable grief. After she dies, Emily is granted permission to relive a day in her life. She chooses her twelfth birthday, and it is in this culminating section of the play that Wilder, like Juntunen, offers the reader/audience simultaneity in terms of time—and finally, a Buddhist-like rendition of letting go. *Our Town* is too often denigrated as simple, homey, and nostalgic. Close reading, however, reveals the play to be much more than a typical "senior class play." Wilder also deals with time, death, and dying in his shorter plays, among them *Pullman Car Hiawatha* and *The Long Christmas Dinner*.

Margaret Edson utilized her hospital work experience in crafting *Wit*. Like Juntunen's protagonist, Edson's character Dr. Vivian Bearing is an English professor who has been diagnosed with terminal cancer. This character, too, uses poetry as she reflects upon her life, in particular the sonnets of John Donne. Edson incorporates flashbacks into the structure of her play. Dr. Bearing, however, has never married, and with the exception of a visit from her mentor—a visit that may be real or in the character's mind—she meets her death with only medical professionals at her side. In the play, faced with the efficient and clinical approaches of the hospital staff (although they are not without compassion), Dr. Bearing learns to blend her intellectual and spiritual sides.

## CAUTION

# THE FIRST YES

CAST OF CHARACTERS
    ERIN—A woman
    RUSS—A man

SETTING—An empty stage

\*\*\*For Russ Tutterow

**AT RISE:** An empty stage. ERIN enters.

ERIN

Erin walked out into her backyard hours before anyone arrived. She wondered if she should have said no to Russ. But, looking around at the lawn and trees, she remembered everything that had happened there. Two Golden Retrievers buried. The dog houses Russ had made for them, scrap lumber in the shed now. Ava jumping through sprinklers during toddler summers. Catching Ava climbing out her window during her teenage rebellion. And all the nights Erin had come outside to look at the stars to find inspiration for her poems. She was a city girl, and the stars out here were always a revelation. But was it worth it? Was all this worth it just because she said yes to Russ all those years ago? Later that night, after people did arrive, she tried to put the question out of her head and to focus on Russ's poetry. Even Ava came home from college, missing her finals week. Once they were all there, milling on the lawn with glasses of Erin's signature mint julep, ice clinking gently in the quiet conversations, Erin stood up on the deck and addressed them.

"Thank you all so much for coming out on this beautiful night to celebrate the release of Russ's new book," she said. "When we got married, there was a sign over our heads that said, 'And their legacy shall be books.' We didn't even notice it at the time, but our photographer captured it, and it encapsulated our

ERIN (con't)

marriage. We all know this book is a special one for Russ. And most of you know I didn't want him at this party tonight. Maybe I should have never said yes to him." She didn't mean to voice that question.

(RUSS enters.)

RUSS

A couple months earlier, Russ came out in the yard to try to get some peace.

ERIN

"You can't just walk out in mid-conversation!"

RUSS

"I thought we were done."

ERIN

"Apparently that's what you want. To just be done with us."

RUSS

"It doesn't seem like I have a choice."

ERIN

"Of course you have a choice."

RUSS

"That's not what I heard the doctor say."

ERIN

"But your CEA count was dropping and—"

RUSS

"It's spread to my kidneys, Erin."

ERIN

"So there's dialysis and—"

RUSS

"And Lorazepam to stay chill, and morphine for the pain, and chemo for the—"

ERIN

"That's right. There's all that. And me. And Ava. What are you going to tell Ava?" Ava was a senior in college, two states away, in a great liberal arts college, while Russ and I plugged away teaching comp at our big state school, stealing time to write poetry. For this tired, tiring, tiresome life with him I had said yes?

RUSS

But we were both tenured.

ERIN

And we owned the house.

RUSS

And we could come out and look at the stars together.

ERIN

We thought we'd get another dog. There should have been time for at least one more. Maybe two.

RUSS

But now ... What was I going to tell Ava? "What am I going to tell Ava?"

ERIN

"Tell her you're not giving up." It was just three years ago we were standing in this yard after we got her safely off to college.

RUSS

We packed up her stuff in our decades-old Volvo—

ERIN

It's why we never got rid of the station wagon. They're bottomless.

RUSS

And we drove her to that great, beautiful, little school in the middle of nowhere.

ERIN

Only three thousand students, all dedicated, literate, lovely—

RUSS

"I can't believe she picked another cornfield state to live in."

ERIN

"You're just going to have to get over it."

RUSS

"But the diversity you get in an urban setting—"

ERIN

"She's in the dorm. It's done."

RUSS

"At least Lisa is the head of creative writing there."

ERIN

"Ava isn't going to be a creative writer."

RUSS

"I know, but we can have Lisa check in on her."

ERIN

"We're not going to be those parents."

RUSS

"I'm going to be whatever kind of parent I want."

ERIN

"One of those parents that calls the Dean to get a grade change?"

RUSS

"Sure."

ERIN

"You will not."

RUSS

"Did you see her roommate?"

ERIN

"Everyone's first year roommate is crazy. It's part of the experience."

RUSS

"I'm going to call Ava tonight and make sure everything is okay."

ERIN

"She needs to get away from us right now."

RUSS

"If she needs a new roommate, we need to get on that right away."

ERIN

"She'll call us if she needs anything."

RUSS

"Are you saying I can't call my daughter?"

ERIN

"Oh, she's your daughter now? Because I seem to recall carrying her around for nine months without any help from you."

RUSS

"I drove you to the OB-GYN."

ERIN

He did. It was sweet. He came to every appointment with me.

RUSS

It was *our* baby—

ERIN

—he said. Every ultrasound, every sonogram, every scare, every first, he was there, sitting in some chair off to the side that the nurse provided. Everything was different after we saw that first sonogram. As soon as we got home, Russ ran into the backyard. "Come back inside!"

RUSS

"I had no idea they could do sonograms so early!"

ERIN

"Come inside. Let's sit."

RUSS

"We should get a dog, now, so it will be trained by the time the kid's born. We can't just call it 'the kid.' What should we call it?"

                              ERIN
"The brat?"

                              RUSS
"It looked like the gem on top of a ring."

                              ERIN
"Our little gem."

                              RUSS
"We need to start saving for its college—We can't say 'its college.'"

                              ERIN
"His or her college?"

                              RUSS
"Verbose."

                              ERIN
"But accurate."

                              RUSS
"We can call it our little gem."

                              ERIN
"Soon enough we'll know the sex."

                              RUSS
"I need to get life insurance, maybe an IRA—"

                              ERIN
"Hold on, hold on—A dog, life insurance, savings—?"

                    RUSS

"We've got to get ready."

                    ERIN

"Yeah. Prenatal vitamins, Lamaze classes—"

                    RUSS

"I've got to take care of our little gem's future."

                    ERIN

"A gem like a little star inside me."

                    RUSS

"Stars are just dead light shining down on us. God willing, our little gem will outlast us. Our gem is our legacy."

                    ERIN

So it was natural that he'd worry with her at college. I did, too. We got the life insurance. We saved. We drove her to the little ivory tower in the middle of cornfields.

                    RUSS

And I would call her whenever I wanted.

                    ERIN

He didn't though.

                    RUSS

I didn't. That first night, I wanted to, all night.

                    ERIN

But he knew she'd call us if she needed anything.

RUSS

I knew that she wasn't scared to ask us for help.

ERIN

That first August night she was at college, we stood in the backyard, arms around each other, feeling one with the fireflies and stars—

RUSS

And mosquitos.

ERIN

This is why my poetry sells better than yours.

RUSS

Whatever.

ERIN

Yours is too dark.

RUSS

It's accurate.

ERIN

And the house was so quiet without Ava. Quiet for the first time in eighteen years. Like the house had released a sigh and was now breathing so softly we couldn't even hear it. We sat in silence for a long while. Then he said:

RUSS

"Maybe we should get a dog."

ERIN

"Let's wait a few years. I'm still not over the last one."

                              RUSS

And then—

                              ERIN

—just over three years later, with Ava in her senior year—

                              RUSS

—I was glad we didn't get that dog. Because even though the last time we saw the doctor my CEA count was dropping, today we learned that it had spread to my kidneys, and, I hadn't told Erin, but the morphine wasn't working anymore. And I didn't know what to tell Ava.

                              ERIN

"You can't stop treatment. It's Ava's senior year. You want to see her graduate don't you?"

                              RUSS

"Don't be an idiot."

                              ERIN

"Don't call me an idiot."

                              RUSS

"Then don't be a bitch."

                              ERIN

"Fuck you!"

                              RUSS

"The chemo's not working! Dialysis isn't going to fix the problem! Morphine isn't keeping me from feeling pain in my kidneys! Jesus, God, I didn't even know you could feel pain in your kidneys! So I will call Ava and tell her it's taken a turn for the worse, and she better tell her professors that she's going to have to come home at some point before finals to visit her father in the hospice!"

ERIN

"The doctor didn't say anything about a hospice."

RUSS

"Erin. That's where this is going."

ERIN

For this? For this I said yes? "Well, then, we should get Ava out of school right away, go somewhere maybe, that European trip we never took—"

RUSS

"I want to finish my book."

ERIN

"So finish it in Europe."

RUSS

"I'm in pain from morn to midnight. I don't want to be on an airplane for eight hours. I don't want to go anywhere. I want to sit in this yard with you nights, and get my poems done. It'll be the first time I turn in a manuscript early. My publisher will drop dead."

ERIN

"Don't joke. We need to talk to the doctor about all the options."

RUSS

"I need you to read my proofs. It's going to be shit if I don't have my regular in-house editor."

ERIN

"We'll see." But of course I said yes.

RUSS

It's how our lives had been for decades.

ERIN

Teaching five paragraph essay structure during the day.

RUSS

Writing our snatches of verse—

ERIN

—not really verse. No one writes verse anymore.

RUSS

Writing our snatches of writing that self-consciously comments on its own literary qualities—

ERIN

Ugly.

RUSS

But accurate.

ERIN

I'm leaving a question mark by it.

RUSS

And, at night, sitting outside. Under the stars.

ERIN

Until our uninvited guests showed up.

RUSS

Blood in the urine.

                        ERIN
Lower back pain.


                        RUSS
A lump.


                        ERIN
Anemia and fatigue.


                        RUSS
Weight loss, loss of appetite, fevers, and Ava knew.


                        ERIN
I never knew what Russ told her, exactly. But he called her. And she came, even
though it was finals week of her senior year. She said she didn't care. She
needed to be in that backyard with her Dad. Alongside so many of his admirers.
Past students, other poets, even fans, if you can believe poets still have fans in
the twenty-first century. And I stood on the deck and told them:

"We all know this book is a special one for Russ. And most of you know I didn't
want him at this party tonight. Maybe I should have never said yes to him: never
said yes to helping him finish this book, never said yes to taking jobs at this
university, never said yes to anything, ever, in the first place, let alone saying yes
to this party. I wanted him in the hospice, where they could take care of him, not
outside, in the cold—"


                        RUSS
Though it was a warm, early summer night—


                        ERIN
And as I was speaking, trying to give him the best introduction I could before he
read from his new, rather his last, book—

RUSS

It was the ending we'd all seen coming from the beginning. That we should have seen coming from the first yes.

(RUSS exits.)

ERIN

—he quietly slipped away. In the dark. Under the stars. Surrounded by friends, by Ava, and, yes, even by the mosquitos. It was accurate. It was an accurate end. And I couldn't read his lines, they blurred before my eyes—Ava would read her father's words out loud later, both his legacies rolled into one breath—but before she did, I told the crowd about how, after dating for two months, in grad school, getting our MFAs, how he told me:

(RUSS returns.)

RUSS

"Our children would have brown hair."

ERIN

"Okay—too soon."

RUSS

"It's just accurate. Genetics."

ERIN

"This is a summer thing. I have my Fulbright. I'm going to be gone for a year, working at the Bibliothèque Nationale—"

RUSS

"But I'm the man of your dreams."

ERIN

"God, that would be awful."

RUSS

"Why?"

ERIN

"Because it would mean I would dream of you the whole time we're apart."

RUSS

"And I'll dream of you the whole year you're gone. You know it's true. Take my hand. Let's shake on it. We'll dream only of each other."

(RUSS holds out his hand. ERIN hesitates.)

ERIN

This is where I could have said no. But it was already too late.

(ERIN shakes hands with RUSS.)

"Yes. Let's do that."

(Blackout.)

**END OF PLAY**

# Solo Playwriting: An Exercise on Guided Imagery, Memory, and Flashback

1. Think about how Jacob Juntunen incorporated imagery of the stars into his characters' backyard.
2. Select a favorite place and describe it in detail. Use descriptive, sensory words. How did the air feel? What sounds were present? What smells?
3. Think about how, as we move through our days, our present actions make us recall scenes from our past.
4. Describe a scene from your past that might be incorporated as a memory into a play that features you in the present. Now write the scene based on your description, and share.

# For Further Research

Fletcher, Anne. "No Time Like the Present: Wilder's Plays and Buddhist Thought." In *Thornton Wilder: New Perspectives*. Edited by Jackson R. Bryer and Lincoln Konkle, 154–188. Evanston, IL: Northwestern University Press, 2013.

———. "Thornton Wilder's 'Eternal Present': Ghosting and the Grave Body in Act III of Thornton Wilder's *Our Town*." In *Death in American Texts and Performances: Corpses, Ghosts, and the Reanimated Dead*. Edited by Mark Pizzato and Lisa K. Perdigao, 79–98. London: Routledge, 2010.

Kübler-Ross, Elizabeth. *On Death and Dying*. Routledge, London. 1969.

# CHAPTER 14

# David Crespy

PLAYWRIGHT

## *STAMPEDE*

©1999 David Crespy

### PRODUCTION HISTORY

"Stampede" was first read at the WaterFront Ensemble, a theatre company Crespy founded with Andrew Young, Wendy Hammond, and Rosemary McLaughlin, along with actors, directors, and playwrights from Mason Gross School of the Arts at Rutgers University. The play then went on to be staged at the Village Gate One-Act Festival (1990), at the Phoenix Theatre Company (1991), at the William Redfield Theatre, and at the Seventh Seal Ensemble Theatre (1992). It has also been performed at the University of Missouri as part of the Mizzou New Play Series.

CAST OF CHARACTERS
    GASTON
    FRAZIER

    SETTING—A sophisticated yet frowzy café in the East Village on 1st Ave.

# About the Playwright

David Crespy is professor of playwriting, acting, and dramatic literature at the University of Missouri (MU). He founded MU's Writing for Performance program and serves as its co-director. Crespy is also the founding artistic director of MU's Missouri Playwrights Workshop and the president of the Edward Albee Society. His plays have been developed and produced at theatres across the United States, including the Cherry Lane Theatre, River Union Stage, NJ Dramatists, Playwrights Theatre of NJ, Nebraska Repertory Theatre, Primary Stages, The Playwrights' Center, HB Playwrights Foundation, Austin Melodrama Theatre, Jewish Repertory Theatre, Stages St. Louis, First Run Theatre (St. Louis), and Creative Theatre Unlimited. Crespy's articles have appeared in *Theatre History Studies, New England Theatre Journal, Latin American Theatre Review, The Journal of American Drama and Theatre, The Journal of Dramatic Theory and Criticism, The Dramatist, Slavic and East European Performance,* and *glbtq.com.* His books include *Off-Off-Broadway Explosion,* with a foreword by Edward Albee (Back Stage Books, 2003), and *Richard Barr: The Playwrights' Producer,* with a foreword and afterword by Edward Albee (Southern Illinois University Press, 2013). Crespy's book *Lanford Wilson: Early Stories, Sketches, and Poems,* which he coedited with poet Jonathan Thirkield, and with a foreword by Wilson's long-time director Marshall A. Mason, was released in October 2017. His recent writing projects include a stage play *The Sad Girl,* which explores soothsaying and serial murder, and *Wretched Grace,* an original screenplay locating Celtic myths within the contemporary text of alien abduction.

# Form and Style

First written in the late 1980s as a reaction both to the acquired immunodeficiency syndrome (AIDS) epidemic in New York City and to the world of squatting, "Stampede" was created in a creative collaboration with actor/playwright and fellow Rutgers alumnus Eric Kuttner, for whom Crespy wrote the role of Gaston. The role of Frazier was written for Crespy. In the years since, both the world of squatting and the AIDS epidemic have been somewhat romanticized and beautifully portrayed in the musical (now a movie) *Rent*. Contrary to what is portrayed in the musical/ movie, the late 1980s and early 1990s in New York City saw a brutal, emotionally and physically debilitating rebellion against a rather awful and challenging period of gentrification in the East Village. Eventually the developers won that battle, with many on the other side of the issue continuing to maintain that New York City lost an important part of its soul. Similarly, there was, and remains, nothing romantic or beautiful about the spread of AIDS during this time period. For many, the aftereffects of the AIDS epidemic in the United States in the late 1980s and early 1990s continue to be felt, both on a national and on an individual level. In fact, playwright Crespy's father, H. Victor Crespy, died of AIDS in 1995.

It has been over thirty-five years since the Centers for Disease Control (CDC) first released a report about what we now refer to simply as AIDS. This nomenclature, however, was not initially used. As scientists at the CDC scrambled to grasp what was happening, they initially named the syndrome as gay-related immune deficiency, or GRID. This was because the initial cases of a rare cancer known as Kaposi (or Kaposi's) sarcoma were found only in homosexual men living in New York City, Los Angeles, and San Francisco. The name GRID was quickly abandoned when doctors realized that heterosexual intravenous drug users who shared needles, women with infected partners, and patients receiving blood transfusions were at risk. By 1983, the CDC ruled out the possibility of AIDS being transmitted through casual contact via food, water, touched surfaces, and air. By 1984 scientists had identified human immunodeficiency virus (HIV) as the cause of AIDS. None of this information, though, did anything to tamp down national talk of a "gay plague," hurtful and discriminatory talk that persisted well into the 1990s. At the same time, with no cure available, family and friends sat by and watched as loved ones died at an alarming rate. It was not until 1987 that the Food and Drug Administration (FDA) approved the drug azidothymidine (AZT) for use in delaying the onset of AIDS. This opened the door for the development of more effective and aggressive antiretroviral drugs during the 1990s. Nevertheless, the FDA's lifetime ban on gay men giving blood, which was instituted in 1983, was not lifted until 2015.

While "Stampede" offers a window into a particular period in our national history, by no means is HIV/AIDS a thing of the past. Recent data from both the CDC and UNAIDS (the Joint United Nations Programme on HIV/AIDS) indicates that over one million people in the United States are living with HIV, and that one in seven of those persons does not know that he or she has HIV. Moreover, since the beginning of the HIV/AIDS epidemic, nearly seven hundred thousand people in the United States have died from AIDS-related illnesses. In 2015 the Obama White House released its updated National HIV/AIDS Strategy, focusing on the core aims of reducing new HIV infections, reducing HIV-related disparities and health inequities, increasing access to care and improving health outcomes for those with HIV, and achieving a national response to the epidemic (see *avert.org* for more about this). Globally, approximately forty million people are living with HIV and seventeen million of those people are receiving antiretroviral medicines. The CDC estimates that over one million people died from AIDS-related illnesses in 2015.

## Plays for Further Study

William H. Hoffman's 1985 Drama Desk Award-winning play *As Is* takes us through the life journey of a gay man who has contracted the AIDS virus, and how he finds support in his former lover. This is one of the first plays that dealt directly with the mystifying malady. Also centered on the rise of HIV/AIDS in New York City in the early 1980s, *The Normal Heart* by Larry Kramer follows writer Ned Weeks's attempts to nurse his partner back to health from an unknown illness thought to be caused by a virus. As the death toll increases and the status of the illness rises to epidemic proportions, Ned pulls together an awareness-raising organization and pleads with government officials to do something. While produced Off-Broadway in 1985, *The Normal Heart* did not premiere on Broadway until 2011. *The Destiny of Me* (1992) continues to follow Ned Weeks. Having lost his lover and having tested positive for HIV himself, Ned begins treatments. Tony Kushner's 1993 *Angels in America: A Gay Fantasia on National Themes,* is a complex examination of homosexuality and AIDS in US culture during the 1980s. Winner of the Drama Desk Award, the Tony Award for Best Play, and the Pulitzer Prize (among others), the two-part play (*Millennium Approaches* and *Perestroika*) has been made into an opera and an HBO movie. Originally conceived as a one-man show, *The Night Larry Kramer Kissed Me* by David Drake uses interconnected scenes to explore AIDS and growing up gay in the late 1980s and early 1990s. Paula Vogel's 1992 Obie Award-winning *The Baltimore Waltz* was inspired, in part, by the loss of her brother Carl to HIV/AIDS in 1988. This **hybrid play** (one that utilizes a mix of elements from both Realism and non-Realism) traces the travels of the characters Carl, an unemployed librarian, and his sister Anna, a schoolteacher who has recently contracted the fatal Acquired Toilet Disease, which is ravaging elementary schools around the country. We eventually learn that their exploits are all Anna's fantasy as she desperately searches for ways to connect with a brother dying of AIDS. *Jeffrey* (1993), by Paul Rudnick, is about a thirty-something gay man in New York who decides to live a celibate life after his sex-filled past. Unfortunately for him, shortly thereafter Jeffrey meets the perfect guy, Steve, at the gym. The rest of this thoughtful comedy wrestles with issues of life, death, and hypersophisticated society in New York City. David Rabe's *A Question of Mercy: Based on the Essay by Richard Selzer* (1996) shares the struggles of Thomas and Anthony as they work through Anthony's final battle(s) with AIDS.

In reading "Stampede," we are also struck by the way Crespy at times uses poetic, if not heightened, language as part of his storytelling. If you are interested in exploring these aspects further, begin with Shakespeare's plays. If you have never experienced reading a Shakespeare play, *The Tempest* might be a good place to start. Eric Overmyer's *On the Verge* (1988) features three Victorian sojourners and a Yeti, among others, while *The Love Song of J. Robert Oppenheimer,* by Carson Kreitzer, explores the question "Do I dare disturb the universe?". Both of these plays have wonderful moments of heightened, poetic language crafted for the contemporary theatre. Other playwrights to consider reading if you are interested in the use of heightened, poetic language would be Mac Wellman, Len Jenkin, Constance Congdon, Sarah Kane, and Naomi Iizuka.

## CAUTION

# STAMPEDE

CAST OF CHARACTERS
GASTON—A grizzled, young poet
FRAZIER—A perfectly composed, young dandy

SETTING—A sophisticated yet frowzy café in the East Village on 1st Avenue.

**AT RISE:** It is Valentine's Day. GASTON, a short bearded, grizzled young poet with a terminally annoyed composure dines with FRAZIER, a perfectly composed young dandy who, at every odd moment, writes elegantly on his napkin. GASTON has a slight Brooklyn accent. FRAZIER took too many elocution lessons for his own good.

GASTON

(Nasty)
Stop it. I said stop it, Frazier. You're doing it again.

FRAZIER

Am I? Yes, I think I am. Sorry.

GASTON

Every damn minute you're writing.

FRAZIER

I don't want to.

(FRAZIER sips a glass of red wine.)

GASTON

Just cut it out. For a second.

FRAZIER

(Writes some more)
There. Sorry, I couldn't help myself.

GASTON

Let me see it.

FRAZIER

No.

GASTON

Oh, give it to me. I've read everything you've written anyway.

(Reads out loud.)

So winter glides to me, in jagged jealousy
as a static signal of snow, blurring my eyes
and grim muffled faces darting despised
pass the stuffy microcosm of this cafe.

(Snorts.)

What the hell does that mean? Huh? It's code. You're fucking writing in code again. God, I hate that. You know what you are? You're a disease. A fucking incommunicable walking disease.

FRAZIER

You're jealous.

GASTON

Oh, yes, let's truck out that same sad old tune.

FRAZIER

You are. And you're not eating.

GASTON

(Quiet)
I hate to eat. I have to force myself.

FRAZIER

You've gotten some tomato sauce on your shirt.

GASTON

So what?

FRAZIER

It's revolting.

GASTON

Oh, yeah?

FRAZIER

(Imitating Gaston)
Yeeah.

GASTON

Okay, fine. Just a minute.

(Stands up, arranges himself and screams painfully.)

THEY'RE ALL JUST A COCKROACH SOUFFLE
THE CONSERVATIVES GROW BOILS AND POP THEM

GASTON (con't)
IN OUR FACES SO WE CAN SEE JUST HOW PAINFUL
LIFE CAN BE WHEN YOU ARE FREE TO EAT ALL
THE MONEY HARD WORK CAN GET!! IF YOU DON'T BELIEVE ME
TURN AROUND AND LOOK AT THE WOMAN BEHIND YOU
WHO HAS GOTTEN FATTER AND FURRIER IN THE LAST
FIVE MINUTES, WHOSE GOLD NECKLACE HAS GROWN
DIAMONDS AND WHOSE TEETH ARE ALL FUCKING CAPPED
WITH THE SKIN OF VERY SMALL BABIES.

FRAZIER
I wish you wouldn't do that.

GASTON
AND MY DINING PARTNER, FRAZIER
WISHES THAT THE PUKE IN MY MIND WOULD
JUST FREEZE UP SO IT WOULDN'T COME POURING
OUT OF ME EVERY TWELVE MINUTES AND FIFTEEN SECONDS.

(Sits down promptly, relaxed, smiling.)

God, I feel better.

FRAZIER
Gaston, couldn't you wait until I left.

GASTON
Every twelve minutes and fifteen seconds. I wish I could stop, Frazier. I wish I could. But I can't and you can't make me.

FRAZIER
It is making less and less sense each time you do it.

GASTON

People understand me, Frazier. They understand and think about what I have to say. You don't like it? Leave.

FRAZIER

You know I can't.

GASTON

Why?

FRAZIER

The lease is in your name. I can't afford another place in the city.

GASTON

So, move to Jersey.

FRAZIER

Poets die in New Jersey.

GASTON

You're not a poet, Frazier, you're a pretentious asshole.

FRAZIER

You don't love me.

GASTON

Of course I love you. What the hell are you talking about. I have to provoke you. Don't ask stupid baited questions.

FRAZIER

All the time.

                              GASTON
What.

                              FRAZIER
All the time? Do you have to provoke me all the time?

                              GASTON
Yes.

                              FRAZIER
I'm trying to eat.

                              GASTON
        (Smiling, warm)
You pretentious fuck.

                              FRAZIER
        (Just as pleasant)
Right now?

                              GASTON
You've got it.

                              FRAZIER
Right now?

                              GASTON
C'mon, baby, taste my sugar.

                              FRAZIER
You're a weak person, Gaston.

GASTON

Allez! Allez!

(*** THEY both stand, look at each other intensely and speak simultaneously, thrusting and parrying with their language.)

*** GASTON

Subliminal dexterity forces me I sense the AIDS in your blood has broken the lovely vase of your spirit. Walls shut you up in your cramped little pipe cleaner body. Have you thought about screaming today. Might do you some good to give serum blood screams to yell out I am a fucking human being not an immoral statistic on your TV.

*** FRAZIER

A bead of sweat swims down your brow in perpetual logic moving wormlike leaving a queer trail of gleaming irony. Can you hear screeching rubber squeals as indifference swells, a soft bump when the cars noiselessly strike a small Siamese that struck and struck still lives claws slicing the air, cutting mortal capers in kitty hijinks and a little girl laughs at this.

(THEY both sit down, relieved, staring at each other, smiling slightly.)

GASTON

I think you won.

FRAZIER

You did.

GASTON

No, it was you this time.

FRAZIER
(False modesty)
No.

GASTON
Oh no, it was you this time.

FRAZIER
No, no.

GASTON
(Peevish)
You won, shithead.

FRAZIER
No, really. It was you.

GASTON
YOU WON YOU WIMPY SVELTE HANDSOME ARROGANT NO TALENT GOD!

(A pause.)

FRAZIER
It <u>was</u> me, wasn't it?

GASTON
Not by much. The kitty was a nice metaphor.

FRAZIER
It's behind you.

GASTON

Really?

   (Turns and looks.)

So it is. Poor little thing.

FRAZIER

See, its tail is still moving.

GASTON

That's sick. Someone should put it out of its misery. I hate suffering.

FRAZIER

You make me suffer.

GASTON

You love it.

FRAZIER

   (Smiling)

I do.

   (Writes a little.)

Ooooh.

GASTON

Good?

FRAZIER

Oooooh. Yes.

GASTON

Let me see.

FRAZIER

No.

GASTON

You let me see when I ask you to let me see.

FRAZIER

You don't have to talk to me that way. You know I'm dying.

GASTON

We're both dying. Don't bring up the obvious. Let me see what you've written. I'm really curious.

FRAZIER

Why don't you eat something?

GASTON

I'm not hungry. I'm never hungry.

FRAZIER

You have to eat.

GASTON

Why? Am I going to die if I don't eat? Well, I'm going to die if I do eat and I'm going to die no matter what I do so why the hell do you have to pester me like my fat godless materialistic mother who lives in Long Island and is going to live to be two hundred and live a miserable, boring useless existence in the meantime I'm going to die at age 35 a horrible death and so are you so don't talk to me about eating, okay?

FRAZIER

I think you don't need to breathe. That's how you go on like that with your language.

GASTON

Wrong. I breathe through my ass.

FRAZIER

Biologically impossible and disgusting at the same time.

GASTON

You are such a pissy bitch, aren't you?

FRAZIER

I've told you about that language. It's inarticulate. Anyway, why do you have to yell your poetry? Why don't you write it down?

GASTON

I can't spell.

FRAZIER

Get a word processor.

GASTON

I can't type.

FRAZIER

Write it down.

GASTON

I don't have enough time.

FRAZIER

Get a nice pen and a smooth white piece of paper with blue lines and write it down.

GASTON

I don't write fast enough to write down all my ideas and anyway a person won't experience my words any better reading them than they would having me yell it in their fucking ear—so I'm going to yell in their fucking ear. You write—you beautiful trite little whatever you are.

FRAZIER

(Writes something down)
There. And that. And that.

GASTON

Give it to me.

FRAZIER

Let me pull it together.

GASTON

Don't play with it!

(Pushes FRAZIER's hand away.)

You always play with the words. You ruin them. Let me see.

(Pulls the napkin out of FRAZIER's hand, reads.)

We spar with tiny adjectives, shiny and hard
breaking our noses into mashes of red
We knife ourselves with alphabet scalpels
into simultaneous stunned bluntness

                              GASTON (con't)
gentle vacuity like the salad on my plate
or the half empty half and halves
plastic and violated next to our coffees.

        (Wads up the napkin and sticks it in his coffee.)

Code.

                         FRAZIER

What?

                         GASTON

But good code.

                         FRAZIER

I wish you wouldn't destroy my poetry.

                         GASTON

Do you want to be read when you've died of the plague?

                         FRAZIER

I … don't know.

                         GASTON

Oh, for Christsake, you want to be a dead poet?

                         FRAZIER

I want to be famous.

                         GASTON
        (Violently spits on the floor in front of FRAZIER)
For what? Kissing up to fucking conservatives and fascists?

FRAZIER

Everything is political.

GASTON

Everything.

FRAZIER

Is it political to get up in the morning?

GASTON

You're saying the world is worth waking up to.

FRAZIER

But you can't help but wake up.

GASTON

Try hemlock the night before.

FRAZIER

Do you want to be another poet suicide?

GASTON

I'd rather vomit. I hate tragic endings. They are such bullshit.

FRAZIER

What are you going to do this evening, Gaston?

GASTON

Call my mother. Work Fourteenth and Broadway. Spend the cash on some blow.

FRAZIER

That doesn't help.

GASTON

I'm dysfunctional. I'm codependent. I've got the plague. Let me have a few laughs before pneumonia or KS kicks in. Jesus, Frazier, you've got it too?

FRAZIER

I carry it. I don't have it and neither do you.

GASTON

You've stopped writing.

FRAZIER

You use it for an excuse for everything.

GASTON

Would you write something?

FRAZIER

(Puts his pen down)
When we met you loved life. I mean you still screamed a lot but you were a more positive screamer. Now …

GASTON

What do you want me to do? I'm scared. I'm always scared.

FRAZIER

You're scared of dying? Excuse me, but the Gaston I know has always looked forward to death, hungrily. A violent painful death.

GASTON

Well, I still do. I like the idea of dying. Even dying horribly. I want to be so repulsive and offensive looking that every fucking Republican fascist Nazi pig and catholic priest will want to puke. I want them to feel every painful fucking thing that I do through visual assault.

FRAZIER

Then what are you scared of?

GASTON

(Pauses)
That you'll die first.

(Pauses.)

Then maybe I'd have to give in and kill myself.

(THEY both are silent.)

FRAZIER

(Instantly touched)
You never say things like that, Gaston.

GASTON

(Rolls his eyes)
You're going to cry, aren't you? What a sissy!

FRAZIER

You shouldn't say things like that.

GASTON

Believe me it's the last time.

FRAZIER

(Writes on his napkin)
Oh, I'm feeling so odd.

GASTON

Let me read it.

                                        FRAZIER
No, you'll spoil it.


                                        GASTON
Give it to me.


                                        FRAZIER
No.


                                        GASTON
Give it to me, or I'll kick your ass in.


                                        FRAZIER
Violent little jerk aren't you?


                                        GASTON
Give me that poem.


                                        FRAZIER
NO!


                                        GASTON
          (Grabbing for it)
Give it!


                                        FRAZIER
Let go. No!


                                   GASTON
          (Grabs it violently out of FRAZIER's hands)
Got it!

FRAZIER

You are cruel.

GASTON

(Reads it. Horrified.)
Love poem.

FRAZIER

(Weakly)
I know.

GASTON

(Now furious, stands up)
LOVE IS FUCKING NEUROTIC NEEDY BULLSHIT
THAT WE SQUEEZE OUT TOWARD EVERY SNEEZING
MISERABLE SQUEALING PORKER FATASS SLEAZOID
WEAK-KNEEDING ACCOUNTING MAJOR AT NYU
WHO GIVES US OUR DAILY FIX OF FLAGELLATION
AND COPULATION AND THE GIRLS WHO WANT IT
SO BAD ARE THE ONES WHO HATE IT THE WORST
WHEN THEY GET IT. LUV, LUV, LUV, ALL THAT
MAKES THE WORLD REALLY SUCK. LUV, LUV, LUV,
LET'S LIVE WITHOUT IT CAUSE IT COMPLICATES
THE FUCK OUT OF THINGS AND THIS LITTLE
SQUIRMY MEALY MOUTH ROMANTIC THINKS HE LOVES ME
WHEN ALL HE REALLY LOVES IS A GOOD KICK IN THE
TEETH A SLAP ON THE BACK OF HIS HEAD AND A
BROOMSTICK UP HIS PIMPLY FUCKING ASS.

(Quietly.)

That was for you. Next declaration in twelve minutes and fifteen seconds.

                                    FRAZIER
        (Crying)
That was the nicest one you've ever done for me.

                                    GASTON
I knew you'd fucking like it. I knew you would.

        (Takes FRAZIER's love poem and holds it over the flame of their table's
        candle.)

And here goes yours.

                                    FRAZIER
Read it first.

                                    GASTON
No.

        (HE burns it. FRAZIER pulls it out of his hand, reads it.)

                                    FRAZIER
        (As GASTON tries to grab it)
No coffee was spilt it was steaming
the stiff vapors made nostrils so wide
and eyes soon followed, softened like eggs
the woozy nodding like the bear in rear car window
bouncing agreeing the silent embrace
the warmth so wet and entrancing
and with it sighs like swollen wind seething
grasping every ventricle the pump shudders
we hear the nothing like it was played on a record
and our innards glisten and shift so easy
it is undeniable and our dying is

                    FRAZIER (con't)
an east village night in summer's august
with your mother to call and my laundry to fold
and a scream and a scream and a laugh

                    GASTON
     (Smiles in spite of himself)
You never read your poems out loud.

                    FRAZIER

It's a piece of shit, wouldn't you say?

                    GASTON

Yes. Code. Boring little pictures and code only you can understand.

                    FRAZIER

But you like it.

                    GASTON

I love everything you write, you arrogant girly asshole.

                    FRAZIER

I love you, Gaston.

                    GASTON
     (Warm and evil)
Don't expect me to say the same to you.

                    FRAZIER

No.

     (Frowns as HE looks at GASTON.)

Hmm.

GASTON

What.

FRAZIER

Gaston, you have a hair growing out of your nose. It's disgusting.

GASTON

Why don't you pull it out with your teeth you miserable, pretty-girl, self-important … only thing in my life.

> (Pauses, gives an angry grunt and a roar.)

I HATE VALENTINE'S DAY! I REALLY DO.

> (HE sits. HE pulls the poem out of FRAZIER's hand and burns it. FRAZIER begins to write again.)

What are you writing?

FRAZIER

Nothing.

GASTON

Let me see it.

FRAZIER

> (Smiles)

No.

GASTON

Give it to me!

FRAZIER

No.

(THEY continue arguing and begin to wrestle over the poem as the lights fade.)

## END OF PLAY

# Solo Playwriting: An Exercise on Historical Inspiration

1. Locate a copy of the November 1990 issue of *Life* Magazine. If this is not readily available to you, then refer to the website: https://changingthefaceofaids.wordpress.com/the-last-days-of-david-kirby/.
2. Look for the photo of David Kirby as taken by Therese Frare.
3. Study the image closely. You should see four people in the image. Read the related stories.
4. Having done this, focus on Kirby's haunting stare. Write what you think might be his inner monologue based on the circumstances you see and have read about so far.
5. Now shift to his sister, and write her inner monologue about the moment.
6. Share.

# For Further Research

Bordowitz, Gregg. *The AIDS Crisis Is Ridiculous and Other Writings, 1986–2003*. Edited by James Meyer. Cambridge, MA: MIT Press, 2004.

Francis, Dennis A., ed. *Acting on HIV: Using Drama to Create Possibilities for Change*. Rotterdam, Netherlands: Sense Publishers, 2011.

Juntunen, Jacob. *Mainstream AIDS Theatre, the Media, and Gay Civil Rights: Making the Radical Palatable*. New York and London: Routledge, 2016.

Roman, David. *Acts of Intervention: Performance, Gay Culture, and AIDS*. Bloomington: Indiana University Press, 1998.

Shilts, Randy. *And the Band Played On: Politics, People, and the AIDS Epidemic*. 20th anniv. ed. New York: St. Martin's Griffin, 2007.

# Credits